Reptiles on Caffeine

Brooke S. Musterman

Warren Publishing, Inc.

Published by Warren Publishing, Inc.
www.warrenpublishing.net

ISBN: 978-1-886057-17-3

Library of Congress Control Number 2008942268

Printed in the United States of America

17039 Kenton Drive
Cornelius, NC 28031

This book is dedicated to Kari Bates,

the most non-reptilian person I have ever met.

Acknowledgements

To Mom, Dad, Steve and Yvonne Musterman, for their constant support and encouragement. I don't think this would have happened without you.

Grandma Sine and Grandma Musterman for their support and encouragement.

Leila and Elizabeth Watkins for their invaluable help in making this happen.

Lindsey Triplett for doing a fantastic job of editing. Adam Martin for your invaluable counsel.

Elli Schulz, Kelly Yeager and Christel Sarchet for being some of the first to read this work and tell me that is was worthwhile to continue. Lauren Spiewak for your constant encouragement.

To everyone else who encouraged me through this process …thank you.

I've always had an affinity for coffee, even when I was young and couldn't take the strength of it. My parents were tea drinkers, so it was rather foreign and exotic to me. It seemed very sophisticated. My grandparents were all heavy coffee drinkers. I remember imagining, while feeding my dog, that I was harvesting coffee and that the dog food was coffee beans in a huge crate, as I had seen the harvesters do. So perhaps that should have served as a sign of the future, or maybe an omen, depending on how you look at it.

Reptiles on Caffeine

People are strange. I'll say it again, people are strange. Not one individual person but people collectively. This is a firsthand, in-depth look at the behaviors most people have a tendency to overlook. Very little of this is exaggerated. These behaviors are based on real-life encounters and are perhaps a prime example of the phrase "truth is stranger than fiction."

This work was originally intended to highlight the various and random "quirks" that we all have, but in "gathering" my quirks I ran into a theme: the majority are stress related. When reading this book, keep in mind that the bustling Café can be a pretty high-stress environment, not just for the employees, but for the customers as well.

The Café is located in a large city, in a tiny, tucked-away spot convenient to both corporate folks who frequently stop by on their breaks to renew their energy for that "next deal," as well as neighborhood folks. Mothers or babysitters drop by, either with kids in tow for a jolt of some much needed energy, or alone as an escape. Kids come by after school to do homework or "hang out." Speed is of the essence at the Café, and whenever speed is expected, stress is involved. Both customers and employees feel not only the personal stress that they

1

are carrying with them that day but also the added stress that comes when more and more impatient people join the already long line.

Our response to fear or stress (of any level) comes from the brainstem, a.k.a. the "reptilian brain." When we are acting within our brainstem, we are not thinking, but merely reacting by instinct or involuntarily (trust me, this is actually a good thing, given the right context). With the Café being a high-stress environment, the employees, as well as the customers, are very prone to reptilian behavior and aggression. This is an examination of both human nature and our reptilian responses to the stressors we encounter in everyday life.

Inferiority Complex

The first and most rampant pathos I encountered was the inferiority complex; a curious thing, the inferiority complex. There is no one who is immune. It is interesting to see the different ways we deal with our own which can range from the downright obnoxious to the sublime acceptance (i.e. "Oh well. Everyone has to be bad at something."). Perhaps the reason it intrigues me so is that I suffer from it as well. To be honest, I found it refreshing that I was not the only one.

The general malaise with the inferiority complex is a feeling of not measuring up to the standard, whatever that may be: a promotion at work, a personal goal, or rejection from a significant other. All sorts of circumstances feed this state of mind.

Inferiority renders it impossible to have a peaceful and stress-free existence. People have one common goal. They basically just want to get along in life. The ways in which they go about achieving this is what causes the great divides between us.

3

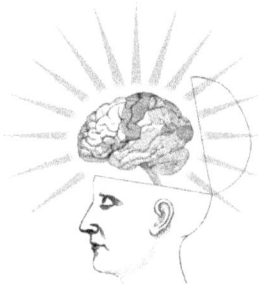

Brainstem Alert

Susan Dunn, M.A., provides some examples of reptilian behavior in the workplace.

1. Hitting your partner instead of hitting the in-box.

    *   Know how to manage your anger and the anger of others.

2. Banging the law clerk instead of banging the gavel.

    *   Hire the best candidate, not the spandex mini.

3. Stealing from the staff lounge refrigerator instead of stealing the competitive edge.

    *   Hunger is a basic instinct, but stealing is stealing. This issue is a major cause of daily stress in many offices.

4. Defending your turf instead of defending the merits of your proposal.

    *   Choose the alternative that will bring results, not the one your ego's riding on

5. Losing a client or sale because you "lose it."

   - Pain, physical and emotional, can also cause us to do things "without thinking."

6. Firing a good worker because you're "on fire."

   - The office thermostat causes a lot of stress in offices. When it gets too hot, we get groggy, then we are prone to anger and violence.

7. Freezing in the middle of your keynote speech.

   - The brain can't differentiate between what's real and not real. Speaking isn't life-threatening. It isn't even dangerous, but many of us act as if it were.

8. Pounding your chest instead of pounding the pavement.

   - Posturing rarely gets you what you want. Instead of bellowing, strutting, and bluffing, try honest communication and empathy.

9. Snoozing and losing.

   - Sleep is primal; get enough, or you'll be dozing off in meetings.

10. Shooting up instead of shooting up the corporate ladder.

- Addictions reside in the reptilian brain. Please get help if you need to. Passing out at the client-company picnic will ruin your career, and alcohol will ruin your life.[1]

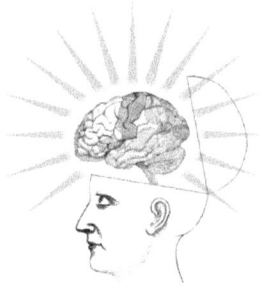

Brainstem Alert

Mike is an individual who is, perhaps, the most prime example of the reptilian brain (and unfortunately he was an authority figure in the Café for a while). It's fairly obvious within the first five minutes of talking to him that he finds his self-worth in his intellect. He is smart-alecky, unpleasant, and often has a perpetual sour look on his face (when he's around people he doesn't like, which is most people). This is the coping mechanism he uses to keep distance between him and others. And believe me, it works! He has an incredible memory which he uses to his advantage.

Mike can never be wrong. The annoying thing is that he rarely is. His two best friends are logic and application. It is no secret how smart he thinks he is, or how illogical, (not to mention stupid) he thinks you are.

It was extremely interesting to work with Mike, albeit infuriating, just to see what would happen next. I found him to be very controlled, very deliberate. For instance, Mike would attempt to be "zany and fun," and for the most part he was successful. The people who were around him several hours of the day knew that he was a glutton for control with rigorous, obsessive tendencies. The interesting thing, and probably very important to point out, was that he was "glutton for control" of the situation and not necessarily the people. The people just kind of got in the way, as they were, or at least contributed to the situation.

He was incredibly smart, maybe to his detriment, if that's possible. He had lots of trouble relating to others.

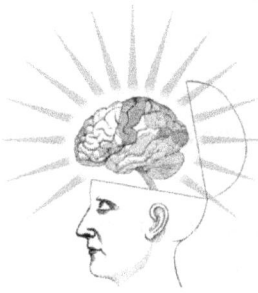

Brainstem Alert

Beth was 23 when she started at the Café. She felt insecure because all her other friends had or were close to having what she considered "a real job." Most of her co-workers were younger than her and was working at the Café just to get through school. She would constantly remind everyone (and herself) that she didn't belong there. She was working toward a "real job." This idea even manifested itself by causing her not to train properly so that she wasn't as skilled as everyone else.

Beth wasn't where she wanted to be or where she thought she should be in life. She took this out on others and was often unpleasant to work with. She was aiming her fury at the wrong people.

"So what's wrong with going through life with only a brainstem?"
- Clyde the Goldfish[2]

"Most people don't give the brain stem a second thought, as it controls things we don't usually have to think about; i.e. breathing, blood circulation, and digestion, to name a few. They have no idea how powerful it can be."

The Brainstem, or Reptile Brain, is also the Survival Brain. "It controls all functions responsible for our survival – as an individual and as a species. It controls such things as hunger, thirst, heartbeat, breathing, digestion, immunity and sexual drive. It is the basic, primal part of us that is in all animals – Give Me Food...Give Me Shelter...Give Me Sex...it (also initiates the Fight-or-Flight Stress Response)." [3]

Describing the brain as a walking tour, Debra Niehoff, Ph.D., says of the brainstem, in her book, *The Biology of Violence*, "Such a tour might begin at the hinge between the back of the head and the neck, where the most posterior portion of the brain, *the brainstem*, meets the spinal cord. This is the historic area, home to ancient neighborhoods bearing majestic Latin names and charged with the organization and management of the enduring functions of daily life: breathing, heart rate, digestion, sleep, consciousness. When a hand brushes your face or you bite your lip while composing a difficult paragraph, sensory nerve endings in your hands, legs, and joints carry similar messages to the spinal cord. Directives flowing in the opposite direction operate the muscles you use to speak, chew, roll your eyes, and turn your head." [4]

"It is very difficult to imagine a lonelier and more emotionally empty being than a crocodile."
- Paul MacLean[5]

The brain stem, or reptilian brain (this brain is an exact replica of the entire brain of lizards and other reptiles), is our primary defense system. When we are in "brain stem mode," we are in primal survival mode. No reasoning is found in the brain stem, as reasoning requires higher, cerebral brain functions. We only have three courses of action to impending doom: fight, flight, or freeze.

Babette Rothschild, who is affiliated with International and European Societies for Traumatic Stress Studies National Association of Social Workers (USA), explains, "These nervous system responses - fight, flight and freeze - are survival reflexes. If perception in the Limbic System is that there is adequate strength, time and space for flight, then the body breaks into a run. If the Limbic perception is that there is not time to flee, but there is adequate strength to defend, then the body will fight. If the Limbic System perceives that there is neither time nor strength for fight or flight and death could be imminent, then the body will freeze. In this state, the victim of trauma enters an altered reality - it is one form of dissociation. Time slows down and there is no fear or pain. In this state, if harm or death do occur, the impact is not so great. People who have fallen from great heights, such as over cliffs, and survived, report just such a reaction. This freezing response may also increase chances of survival. If the cause of the freeze is an attack by man or beast, the attacker may lose interest when the prey has gone dead, as a cat will lose interest in a lifeless mouse.

It is important to understand that these Limbic System/Automatic Nervous System responses are instinctive, not chosen by thoughtful consideration, but are reflex actions." "When someone insults our ego, for instance, we feel threatened and become angry or retaliate, even though we have not been physically harmed. If the boss tells us to come in to his office, our first fear is that we're going to be fired, so we become defensive. It's our source of sustenance, after all: food and clothes for our children."[6]

"When encountering such perceived threats, we can be "hijacked." Our reptilian responses are strong and designed to supersede thinking. They are automatic. After all, if a roaring lion is headed your way, you don't want to stop to figure out what species it is. Your reptilian brain pumps out the chemical of "fight or flight" so you will act, immediately, without thinking.

In the face of danger [or the mere perception of danger], there are two sorts of reactions out bodies can display:

1. A Conscious sensation or reaction - by the cerebrum or new brain - takes about 1.5 to 2 seconds.

2. An Unconscious sensation and reaction - by the cerebellum or old brain - is around 10 times faster.

Therefore, since we are not using our higher brains when we are reacting, we are not 'human-thinking.' We're only human-thinking if we have time to consider."[7]

We may see, and even envy the fast talkers that we encounter everyday. (Why can't we do that?) However we can take some comfort in the fact that they are merely rehearsed reptilian responses.

This is why people like soldiers, firemen, and policemen are trained so that their duties become second nature to them.

They can respond without thinking. But the dark side is, we can also be trained for far les noble defense. Our armor becomes hypocrisy. Our weapons become sarcasm and invalidation. With enough training, these responses, too, soon become second nature. Sometimes it's hard to believe that the part of the brain that causes heroic and even intimidating actions can be responsible for actions that are perceived as dim witted and inept. Reptilian responses would be included in what Dr. Suzanne LaCombe describes as 'activation'. By this, she simply means any bodily response to the nervous system. "Because the source of activation lies in the primitive reptilian parts of the brain—the parts beyond our conscious control-the higher our activation, the less control we have in directing our thoughts, emotions or our behavior."

She explains further, "In other words, higher activation coming from the primitive areas of the brain will interfere with and diminish our capacity to adapt to circumstances as aggressive, inflexible, and territorial reactions. We see the Reptilian Brain in action when people feel emotionally threatened. They become aggressive, defensive, and rigid. We see it in people who are feeling insecure and become 'control freaks'. We see it in turf battles, power struggles, and mindless insistence on doing things 'like we've always done them.' The effects of trauma on the brain pose serious problems for employers who are trying to cultivate a productive workforce. Chronically stressed employees, because of downshifting, end up operating out of their Primitive Brain. Unless we want employees who are acting according to the law of the jungle and who are using a small fraction of their intellectual capabilities, we need to create environments which allow the more intellectually and socially advanced processes of the neo-cortex to be engaged.[7]

David Lee, a noted speaker, consultant, and author on stress in the workplace observes, "We have all experienced Reptilian Brain responses. Two common examples are feeling uneasy when our routine has been interrupted and feeling angry when someone sits in our favorite chair or at our desk without asking. Despite telling ourselves we shouldn't be upset, we are; the survival programs of the Primitive Brain have been activated, sending us signals that something is wrong. When our more sophisticated, intellectually advanced neo-cortical capabilities get overwhelmed; these primitive responses engage; resulting in aggressive, inflexible, and territorial reactions. We see the Reptilian Brain in action when people feel emotionally threatened. They become aggressive, defensive, and rigid. We see it in people who are feeling insecure and become 'control freaks.' We see it in turf battles, power struggles, and mindless insistence on doing things 'like we've always done them.' The effects of trauma on the brain pose serious problems for employers who are trying to cultivate a productive workforce. Chronically stressed employees, because of downshifting, end up operating out of their Primitive Brain. Unless we want employees who are acting according to the law of the jungle and who are using a small fraction of their intellectual capabilities, we need to create environments which allow the more intellectually and socially advanced processes of the neo-cortex to be engaged."[8]

Bestselling author Jeffrey Gitomer lists some of the deadly, not to mention unproductive, effects of stress. Since Reptilian Brain is caused by stress, the words can be used interchangeably.

How do negative thoughts and feelings, dominated by the Reptilian Brain, affect you? They:

> Drain your energy.
> BLOCK positive thought.
> Cause worry.
> Cause illness.
> BLOCK creative thought.

Cause errors.

Reduce productivity.

Cause anger.

Prolong painful situations.

Affect the way you listen to others.

Affect the way you communicate with others.

Affect the way you deal with others.

Take the fun out of your life.[9]

None of these effects are useful in any workplace.

The Café's employee training is similar to a soldier's training only in that we are trained in such a way that the skills become second nature to us so that we don't usually have to think about it. I always "joke" that while I have to be at work at 5 am, I usually don't wake up until around 8 am. This always gets a laugh out of people, but I can honestly testify that during the first few hours of work I am moving out of pure habit and repetition. There is very little thinking involved and I am certain that I am not the only one.

In the article "Balancing the Autonomic Nervous System," Paul Chek explains, "The neurologist Paul MacLean has proposed that our skull holds not one brain, but three, each representing a distinct evolutionary stratum that has formed upon the older layer before it, like an archaeological site: He calls it the "triune brain." MacLean, now the director of the Laboratory of Brain Evolution and Behaviour in Poolesville, Maryland, says that three brains operate like "three interconnected biological computers, [each] with its own special intelligence, its own subjectivity, its own sense of time and space and its own memory". He refers to these three brains as the neo-cortex or neo-mammalian brain, the limbic or paleo-mammalian system, and the reptilian brain, the brainstem and cerebellum (see above diagram). Each of the three brains is connected by nerves to the other two, but each seems to operate as its own brain system with distinct capacities."

Paul Chek goes on to say that Paul MacLean describes the difference between the reptilian brain and the mammalian or human brain as such:

"The mammalian brain and neo-cortical, or human brain structures, [are] outgrowths of the reptilian brain. This is important to understand because many people misinterpret MacLean's model thinking that the individual brain structures are modular, or independent of each other in function, which they are not. The best way to understand the triune brain system is to realize that the reptilian brain is like the operating system of a computer (e.g. Microsoft Windows) – it is the platform upon which all the other computer programs operate. In this case, the other computer programs are the mammalian and neocortical brain structures." [10]

"You-- I could kill you. I mean it. I could rip your head off one- handed and drink from your brainstem."
                                                   - **Spike from *Buffy the Vampire Slayer***

Let me give an example of how easy a thought or attitude can downshift from the limbic brain (rational brain) to the reptilian brain. Everyone will be able to relate to this "reptile attack."

Sally is tidying up the condiment bars. It seems she is doing things in a different order than Alan would prefer. Sally is restocking the sugars, napkins, etc. before wiping the bar down. Alan stops to instruct her (with no animosity at first) to wipe the bar down first before restocking.

Sally, feeling it is more expedient at this particular time to do things in the order that she is, keeps on doing what she's doing.

This apparently borders on infuriation with Alan. What started as a cerebral suggestion quickly turned into an irrefutable reptilian demand. This is a prime example of the downside to our cold-blooded friend; it often makes us, well, cold-blooded.

I'm pretty sure everyone can relate to Alan in this situation. Everyone remembers times when they just "snapped" at even the smallest indignation.

Benefits of the Reptilian Brain

Our brainstem is programmed to act automatically at the mere hint of stress. It is for our benefit, although it may not always seem that way.

Susan Dunn, M.A. explains in *The Tyrannosaurus Rex Rears Its Necessary Head*, "As we sit at a formal dinner worrying about what silverware to use and talking about Van Gogh, our dinosaur friend is right there with us. After all, when someone cuts you off on the highway, the act itself isn't life-threatening, but the chemical your brain pumps out, the stress it causes is life-threatening." [11]

Dr. Suzanne Lacombe, Ph.D, shares a corroborating explanation in *What's With the Reptile?* The brainstem is like a bodyguard who is constantly watching your back, constantly scanning the environment for potential threats. The reptilian brain decides whether it's going to fight or flight because the thinking brain is too slow to protect you when you're suddenly confronted by danger. So when a 90 mile an hour curve ball's coming at you, it's the reptilian brain that reflexively jerks your head out of the way before you even realize what's happening." [12]

Just to reiterate, the reptilian brain is our protective reflex. It can go into overdrive. It reacts without thinking. It lacks the cerebral skills to differentiate between real and perceived dangers. The reptilian brain helps us not only with simple things like eating and procreating, but also to take initiative; to start things. It is essential with structure; i.e. daily routines like scheduling activities, as well as territorial inclinations such as claiming a favorite chair or parking spot or traveling to work the same way everyday. It is what helps us master more difficult routines such as karate or dance.

On a personal level, it is my brainstem that allows me to show up at work half asleep and still pull off a decent work performance, as long as I'm not expected to deviate from my routine. The minute a change in said routine occurs that requires me to think, I can no longer fake it.

Terry Bragg, in his very educational article, "How to deal with clients, bosses, and coworkers who act like reptiles," explains "It is for this reason that, in the Industrial Age, the reptilian brain was honored and needed. Companies expected assembly line workers to take orders and work without thinking. Industrial Age management performed the functions of the neo-cortex. Management did the thinking and workers did what management told them to do.

In the Information Age, this arrangement no longer works. Today, workers must think, make decisions, and use their creativity. In the Information Age, reptilian behavior is a disadvantage and a hindrance. Yet, reptilian behavior still exists."[13]

"I'll need Jack's PC motherboard, the brainstem of a recently dead human, and some 5/8 inch flathead screws. Where am I gonna get 5/8 inch flathead screws at this hour?"

- Mr. Tickles and CJ, "Fuzzy Logic"[14]

Back to the Café: Okay, you ask, why in the world is your brain receiving stress signals in a Café of all places? I know some people are understandably confused when I use the term "threatened" because: a) a Café probably seems to be a very non-threatening place and b) the word "threat" brings to mind all kinds of violent images that are (hopefully) unrelated to most Cafés. However, "threat" comes in all shapes and sizes. I am certainly not talking about physical danger. I am merely talking about threat to performance, speed, and execution (which can send the same kind of "danger" messages to the brain as the threat of impending violence can). Even minor changes can send threatening messages to the amygdala (which is the part of the limbic system which helps process our fear and anger emotions). "We must overcome two basic fears in the workplace: (1) fear of embarrassment and (2) fear of failure. If people are afraid, they will be embarrassed or treated as failures, and they will not take risks. A prime task of management is to create a work environment where people are not afraid of embarrassment or failure."[12]

Perhaps you're asking why are people "threatened" by anything that might be a hindrance to these. Well, perhaps when we are not in the middle of a stressful situation where our performance is not perceived as being challenged or hindered, we can see it as less of a "threat." Trust me, when you get in a high-adrenaline situation where you are just reacting instead of thinking, anything that could impede action is perceived as a possible "threat."

In her review of the television show *The Sopranos*, Victoria Alexander tells us,

"The oldest brain, the reptilian, plays an important role in aggressive behavior, territoriality, ritual, and the establishment of social hierarchies. *The Sopranos is* the celebration of man's evolutionary prerogative: his reptilian brain. This is the real reason why *The Sopranos* is hailed as the best show on TV. We recognize, on an unconscious level, that the show venerates the Reptilian Brain that we all possess, and suppress... Every character operates purely from the Reptilian Brain: 'I want, I want, I want. I want NOW! I want what I think is important to me.'[15]

"*I would rather tear out my brainstem, take it to the nearest four-way intersection, and skip rope with it than go on living where I do now."*

- Carl from *SpongeBob SquarePants*

Walter Cannon, a Harvard Physiologist, discovered what is called the "fight or flight" stress response. It is an actual chemical release the brain sends out. The fight or flight response is innate in all creatures. It is a built-in security system. It is activated from both internal and external stress; real or imagined.

It should be noted that the reptilian stress responses are sent out for our immediate survival. If you are in a situation where you are unable or unwilling to fight back, flight would be your immediate reptilian response. If you are in a situation where you'd rather fight 'til the death than admit that you're wrong, fight would be the immediate response. Since the Café employees have the "flight" option at the risk of their job, it is the "fight "or "freeze" response that is most often employed. We haven't talked much about the "freeze" response. Dr. Suzanne LaCombe discusses this extensively in her article, The Freeze Response. "In the last moments of the chase, when there is literally no possibility of 'fight or flight', the victim will experience the freeze response. It will feign death by 'playing possum'. [16]

Dr. LaCombe proposes that actions such as holding your breath, heaving a deep, long sigh could be construed as the human equivalent to 'playing possum'. The freeze response is hard-wired in our reptilian brain. When 'fight or flight' is not an option, our autonomic nervous system goes into a freeze response and we become immobilized." The phrases' scared stiff' or frozen with fear' reflect this mammalian characteristic. A deer that's 'frozen in the headlights' is responding likewise.

The Innovative Brain newsletter tells us in its article *But Seriously, Nobody's Perfect...or Surrender to Your Humanity.* The article goes on to state, "Less complex animals, like reptiles, have three choices in terms of how they might deal with that 'newness:' kill it, eat it, or run from it....Our natural reaction when confronted with 'newness' is the same to an extent. Fortunately, we have another part of our brain, the neo-cortex (the 'innovative brain') which has the ability to override the primitive instincts of the brainstem. We can treat newness with curiosity. We can defer judgment and look for the possibilities that exist in new ideas. We can be smarter than [reptiles] if we choose to be. Innovation teams are smarter than [reptiles] most of the time (notice we didn't say 'all of the time?'). Creative individuals on innovation teams have re-habituated themselves so that their first response to newness is to understand it fully before they assess its potential value. It's their pathway out of the swamp." [17]

"If you are distressed by anything external, the pain is not due to the thing itself, but to your estimate of it; and this you have the power to revoke at any moment."

- Marcus Aurelius

While Marcus is correct in both his estimation of stress and his remedy for it, he oversimplifies it a bit, methinks. While we do indeed have the ultimate power to revoke stress at any moment, we must fight our innate biology to do so.

I'm sure that everyone would agree that most stress is anticipatory. This is, we are making assumptions about how something will turn out. *I just know that this will be disastrous.* But we really have no concrete idea how the end will turn out. This is actually a pre-wired defense mechanism our brain provides us with. But as with anything, it can be taken to the extreme, which accounts for much of the rampant paranoia and ensuing aggression. This is all too common at the Café; it is foresight gone awry.

The more negative characters presented here are normal, everyday people. (You may even recognize yourself.) For every negative, or reptilian, action presented here, I have probably seen several positive actions to counterbalance them. What, then, causes normal people to act in such manners? Consider a newborn infant: the infant has only its immediate needs in view and is not, in the least bit, concerned with politeness in getting them met. This is how grown folks act when thinking with the brainstem. "No matter what degree of control is exercised by the neo-cortex in terms of morals, ethics, good intentions, etc., when 'push comes to shove' we revert to type – and reverting to type means animal-instinctual. This is clearly verified by the being 'overcome' by rage, fear or sadness and being unable to stop it."

This concept of the automatic nature of the reptilian brain is further validated by Susan Dunn: "The reptilian brain is automatic, outside our control, and sometimes said to be 'unconscious.' What are we to do then? [It is actually very similar to the brain] of the alligator, it won't listen to reason (the neo-cortex), and it doesn't care about anyone (limbic) in comparison to the addiction. We can't call it, push it, or pull it, but we can pick the thing up and move it. And we can keep it where it needs to be. We need muscle to do that, and one of the things that gives us muscle is improving our emotional intelligence and getting conscious." [18]

Several ethological studies have been conducted on aggression and territoriality. Ethology is the term used to describe the study of animal behavior, which has given tremendous insight into the behaviors of humans. One such example is Norwegian behaviorist Schjelderup-Ebbe's experiment with chickens: He compared how many times a chicken pecked other members of the lock to the number of pecks received. This is known as the infamous "pecking order."

These ethological studies were somewhat unpopular among the public, as people didn't like being told that their behaviors were "animalistic." It took away any notion of free will. However, if you observe any animal interactions for any length of time, you will note that all species have some sort of innate territoriality, pecking order and defensive actions pertaining to these ideas. Humans are by no means exempt from this.

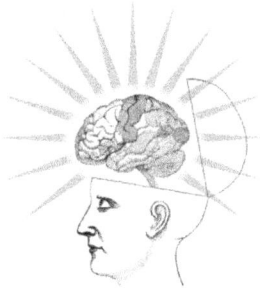

Brainstem Alert

Alan is a very efficient manager. He is well liked and very effective as a leader and organizer. Alan is very fun; however, like anyone else, he likes things done a certain way. His reptilian brain caused him to be narrow-minded and abrasively "always right" in his own mind. He speaks in a demanding tone that makes him sound confrontational even when asking something as innocent as "How are you?" He is slow to change and doesn't have much patience for people who do things differently than him.

I later learned that people were not, in fact, staying up night after night strategically plotting how best to make my life miserable, though it often felt that this was so. I learned that these are valid "quirks." Some people prefer to call it "behaviors" or "personality manifestations." We all have them. I know for a fact that I annoyed them just as much, if not more than they annoyed me.

This leads me to the next common pathos I encountered. With this we will also discuss customer behavior, lest you think I am using this book to simply bash my co-workers. The common name for this is simply "the control freak" (which we learned earlier is quite reptilian). It might also be called an authority complex among other titles. I'm sure we all can name at least one person in our lives who displays this behavior.

This common behavior stems from a need for control because of a lack of control in other areas. There is often no way of knowing what issues are behind these behaviors, but there is no doubt that there are some. Alan presents as being very "in the know," very "I'm in control of this situation," which is no accident.

It's extremely important for Alan to be right and for it to be known that he is right. This is shown by the way he will bring up situations where he has been shown to be right in every day conversation. He vilifies or "bashes" the other person to bring himself up, which is a common tactic of insecure people.

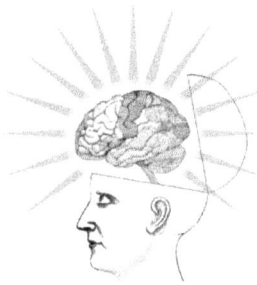

Brainstem Alert

Alan and Cindy are opening the store together, which involves a significant amount of time without customers. So, to fill the silence, Alan talks randomly about family life and he also brings up an incident involving another employee, Tim. It seems Tim wasn't sweeping the floor as effectively as Alan would have preferred.

"I mean, I can't believe he was just brushing the broom around. He wasn't getting anything up. I honestly don't know what he was thinking. If he thinks that's sweeping, he obviously has never swept before."

Alan always assumes the worst about people and rarely apologizes when he is wrong, as he often is. This is a common characteristic of a controller, a sort of "heading off at the pass." In his narrow mind, it was not possible that Tim may have swept the floor before and was just touching up. Tim is a competent employee who has, indeed, swept before; therefore he knows how it's done. It is entirely possible that Tim may have been being lazy, but that's not the only possibility. I think it's much more productive to look at his past track record; the other times he has swept successfully, not to mention the overall look of the floor before you start slandering him in front of other people who have nothing to do with it.

Alan, it seems, cannot give praise without pointing out a fault, which is not only very reptilian, but it shows how insecure he is. I could compliment someone to him, and he would respond, "Yeah, but I don't like the way she..." or "I agree, but he always..."

Jeffrey Gitomer calls this "Limited Self Image through the third person." Gitomer asks, "When someone asks you, 'What do you think about Bill?' do you give your opinion in negative terms -- what Bill can't do -- or where Bill falls short?

On rare occasions you might have nice things to say at the beginning, followed by the word BUT, with 'but' being the downside. 'He's a great guy, but he drinks too much.'

People put others down to build themselves up ... "I believe I'm better than Bill; therefore, I can put Bill down." [19]

Alan suffers from another pathos that I can claim as well: the superiority complex, or "It's all about me" syndrome.

If anyone is having a conversation and Alan is within earshot, he believes he is privy to that information and will usually join in. If he comes in on the tail end of a conversation, he will assume it is about him and immediately get defensive.

25

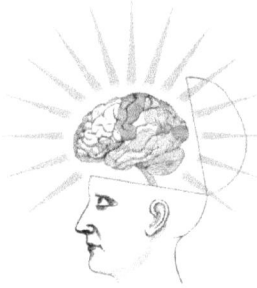

Brainstem Alert

Butch is a customer who I never noticed until the other day, when he snapped and yelled at us for not remembering his drink order. He comes to my register. I say, "Hi. Can I help you?" Butch says, "Medium coffee with room for whole milk."

I am off to retrieve Butch's coffee. I hand it to him, exactly what he asked for. He is immediately upset. I didn't understand that he wanted hot milk in his coffee, as he never told me.

"Look at my face!" he thunders, "I get coffee with WARM milk...I'm in here every day. I don't understand why you can't remember that!"

My first (reptilian) thought was "Okay, Butch obviously has personal issues far beyond anything I can get into here. Apparently he is so self-centered that he thinks that, out of all the thousands of customers I see every hour, I should remember HIS order when he never says anything to me to differentiate himself from the other thousands of people I see every day, although he has no problem with yelling and causing a scene over a simple cup of coffee." (It should be noted that the next day he came in and ordered something completely different.)

I've heard the worst thing you can do to a person is show indifference. I've found this firsthand to be true both on the giving and receiving end. I guess this is just such an instance. Butch felt ignored and in turn took it out on us. Maybe he was having a bad day, and this just pushed him over the edge. I am in no way condoning his behavior, just trying to explain what was behind it.

I am almost ashamed to say that I have often shown indifference on purpose to piss people off, and it does work.

Now, when reading these various accounts it's important to remember that these are normal everyday people, just like you or I. They are not necessarily "mean" people. In fact, I'm sure that there are a lot of people who find them pleasant or nice. In other words, this is not behavior that is indicative of them. I've always found it interesting how "normal" everyday people can just snap given the right circumstance. These people are thinking with their brainstems. It will give you a sense of how powerful the brainstem really is.

I have always been of the opinion that humans are basically selfish. Sure, lots of times we are nice and good, but I don't think that is our basic instinct. Often, any good displayed has selfishness at its core. Not always, mind you, but manners have to be learned; it certainly doesn't come naturally. Think of how quickly a baby or toddler will learn to con people to get their way. My research into the reptilian brain, experience at the Café, and heck, just living through life has only confirmed this.

I have observed, both personally and with other people, co-workers who are super nice and will go out of their way to seemingly accommodate you one minute and use that as an excuse, if you will, to speak disrespectfully to you and about you.

Somehow, this practice is viewed as acceptable. I know about this because I used to do it and used the same sort of logic to excuse it, except, rather than using the "trade off" method (sometimes accommodating them), my excuse (as is everyone who employs this method) was that "they have to learn somehow." The only problem is that they usually don't learn, and if they do, it's more often than not done so grudgingly. I have found that people generally learn better when they are treated with respect.

I realize that we only see a small portion of their personalities, as we don't really know most of these people beyond "Can I take your order?" Brainstem thinking notwithstanding, we don't usually know that these behaviors could really be consistent with their personalities.

Are You Paranoid?

The next pathos I encountered was the "Everyone's pulling the wool over my eyes" pathos, or simply put, "paranoia." This seems to be most common for people in charge. Now, don't misunderstand, I'm not against people in management "checking up" on subordinates or making sure the job is being done well: that is completely appropriate. In fact, it is part of the managing job, but grilling trusted employees (especially during the morning rush) is not only inappropriate but also counterproductive, especially when it is just to show who's in control.

This is not a behavior indicative of just managers, mind you. It goes across the board as well. I've even found it in myself. Let's trace its sordid little path, shall we? It stems from insecurity (the root of all evil), which can lead to a competitive nature. Thus we can start to think that "Everyone is against us," or "I must make others look bad," which conversely can have you looking over your shoulder because you think everyone else feels the same way you do.

This is a behavior displayed in customers as well. Perhaps they are feeling insecure about their job. Maybe they were passed up for a promotion or just having a bad day. One day a regular $1.75 customer decides to get a scone with his coffee one day. I tell him the total: $3.50. He then gets belligerent with me saying, "FOR A CUP OF COFFEE?!"

I explain that the price of the coffee and the scone are more than his normal single cup of decaf. Then he suddenly remembers that he ordered the scone and is extremely embarrassed and apologetic for making such a scene. This sounds like a rare occurrence, but it actually happens more than you would think. They feel they've suffered enough injustices in their day so far without the coffee shop cashier willfully and wrongfully cheating them out of $1.25.

Now let me make my usual disclaimer: I am not against pointing out cashiers' math errors, nor am I pro-overcharging, but it seems to me that there are far more dire circumstances to spend your energy getting upset about.

I've always found it curious to encounter people who are rather cold, bordering on rude, until you start to chat with them. It's normal to me not to be as friendly as you would if you knew the person better, but I find it a tad demeaning when someone can't just be polite before they get to know me. Some people need that, I guess.

We create our own version of reality based on preconceived notions from people's words or actions. This is impossible to change, but we *can* change the suppositions after they're made. We constantly create internal narratives. If a server is quiet (or acts in a manner different from the way you would act), you could assume he's annoyed at you. And he could be, or he may have had a fight with the boss. Perhaps he's shy or attracted to you. It could be any number of things, which may or may not have anything to do with you, but the version of reality you choose to believe about him will shape both your attitude and the way you behave towards him.

Maria is what some might call a high-powered businesswoman. When she first started coming into the Café, I thought she was completely rude.

"Hi. May I take your order?"

"Grande 2% latté," she would respond, all the while looking at her watch like she'd rather be anywhere else. After she received her latté, she would power walk on out the door.

However, when I started chatting with Maria while she was waiting one day, just making small talk, I found her to be a lot less brusque. We even started meeting for lunch fairly regularly.

I have often found, and am sure that others have found towards me, that sometimes not being sure of what to say, for whatever reason, may cause us to perceive someone as rude, when in fact nothing could be further from the truth. Some people just aren't good at small talk and certainly not to people they don't know. Most don't have the chatty personality that I can put on. I say "put on" because it actually isn't my nature to be chatty. I just do it so much for work that I will often "forget" my natural tendencies, but never fear, for they are lurking just beneath the surface waiting to come out and usually at the most inappropriate time. Such as when I'm trying to impress someone for a prospective job or trying to show someone how smooth I can be.

Even though I know this to be true about myself, I can be very intolerant of it in others. It is simply because I often hold others to a higher standard than I do for myself.

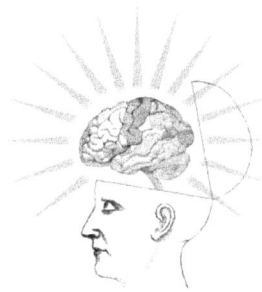

Brainstem Alert

My co-worker Christina me told of a story of which I'm sure everyone can relate to very well. There was a customer named Bob who was kind of quiet. "I actually thought he was kind of a jerk when I first encountered him. He wouldn't smile. He said little else besides giving his order. He just wasn't the chatty type," she told me. While some regular customers like to be recognized and small talked, Bob seemed to prefer anonymity. Christina told me that she misread his quietness for him being standoffish and reacted to him accordingly. She regretfully told me that she would glare at him and keep her conversation to a minimum when he came up to her register. Christina perceived Bob as wanting nothing to do with her (even on the short-term basis with which we encounter people), so she returned the sentiment.

As it turns out, Bob actually is a nice guy. He just is not a talker, which is his right. "I feel bad for acting as I did," she said. "I was trying to force my acquaintance on him," she laughingly said.

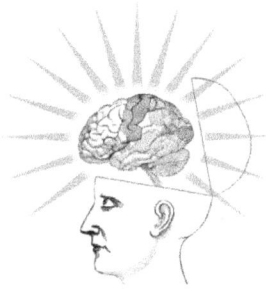

Brainstem Alert

Terrence is flamboyant and fabulously gay. He is seemingly nice on the surface but is bad-mouthing you the moment you are out of earshot. He is well liked, even though no one is exempt from his slander. His meticulous nature makes him hard to work with. It seems he was born with a disapproving eye.

Terrence is obviously insecure about something. What it is I don't know because he seems to be good at everything. He is very likeable, but has a pattern of catty   invalidation that will cut you to your very core.

I always find it so interesting, albeit enraging, how everyday people use invalidation to their advantage and how often they succeed at victimizing us. People you wouldn't think would feel the need to, people who seem very "together." It's almost refreshing once I really dissect it to know that everyone has insecure days, everyone has something that they're not good at.

Invalidation

Invalidation, or bullying, is all too common at the Café. I've studied this extensively and discovered, to my horror, that no one is immune from invalidation. Since invalidation is contagious, everyone invalidates and everyone is invalidated by someone. Very few are actually above it. We do it without even realizing that we are doing it, and often it is done to us without our realizing it.

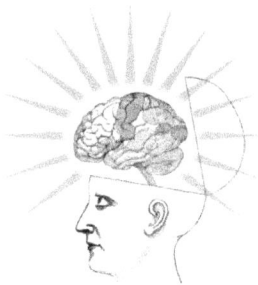

Brainstem Alert

Timothy is a fun supervisor, but I hate working with him because he is so much like me. He is disorganized and always trying to get me to cover a shift at the last minute. He has an annoying habit of invalidating you by making fun of you in a way that is not usually perceived as such, sort of a backhanded compliment. So if you were to complain about it, he could just say something like, "What? I was just trying to give you a

34

compliment." Then you'd look like someone who had a chip on her shoulder.

I've learned a thing or two about invalidation both from experience and from research. A lot of times we don't recognize invalidators. These people are smarmy, controlling, covert operators. You may not be able to pinpoint right away why you feel bad. These people feel so inferior that they need for *you* to feel bad so that they're in control. You may feel only a negative "energy" emitting from them, or maybe you just don't want to be around them for no apparent reason. Many invalidators are oblivious to their poison. It could be entirely unintentional (which doesn't excuse or lessen the impact any).

CASE STUDY

Karl "Go Fly" Roberts is a curious fellow. I never quite understood what made him tick. He was probably in his late 40s to early 50s, if I had to guess. For whatever reason, he has a tremendous affinity for the Philadelphia Flyers. In fact, that is how he got his nickname. The first thing usually out of his mouth (before hello) is "Go Fly!" We at the Café have sort of fallen into the whole routine. When we see Karl, we say, "Go Fly!" as well.

The other funny quirk about Karl is when he asks you how you're doing; here is a typical conversation with Karl:

"Go Fly! Hi Brooke. How are you doing today?"

"Hi Karl. Go Fly! How are you?"

"I'm always good. You know that. There's no reason not to be."

At this point, you have already gotten too much information, but alas, he's still rambling on about the aspects of positive thinking.

This would happen every day, although some days he will go into further detail about how it is up to us to choose our mood. Maybe he's been through a traumatic life-changing experience which has left him with this new appreciation for life, which he feels he must force upon everyone else.

I have seen him eating by himself on several occasions. I think he is lonely, which is quite sad. I also think that this may be his way of compensating.

It also is obviously very annoying. I, for one, don't like people challenging me on anything, much less why I happen to be having a less than perfect day, especially when he can plainly see that we are extremely busy. So the way I've learned to handle Karl is to just parrot back what he says: "Karl, I don't know why you have to ask, because you of all people know I'm doing wonderful—there's no reason not to be." The first few times he was taken aback that I had stolen his line, but now he's used to it, and now he is not the only one who is amused.

Now, I have nothing against positive thinking, I just don't like it forced upon me. Interestingly enough, we all feel that everyone thinks (or *should* think) exactly the way we do which, thank God, isn't true. Similarly, we also think everyone picks up on the same problems or "flaws" that we do, when actually people are usually so focused on themselves that they fail to even notice what we've been obsessing about.

The Hoi Polloi

There are the common, quirky actions that not necessarily related to reptilian brain, perhaps, besides the fact that they are behaviors that they ALWAYS display, such as, the lady who orders the caramel macchiato "with whipped topping" everyday, even though we've repeatedly explained to her that it is real whipped cream.

Why in the world do people feel they must leave a modern art style mural of creamer, sugar, Equal wrappers, stir sticks, and napkins? Weren't we all raised to clean up after ourselves? Even I, a self- and (other-) proclaimed slob, know better than to leave trash less than two inches from the wastebasket without making a less-than-concentrated effort to dispose of it properly.

Another common curious behavior is the "I'm a regular" complex. Believe me; this is far different from the "true" regulars who have several months/years of coming in under their belt. These are the people like Mara who act like we should bow down at their feet when they come in and was doing this after only a few weeks. I realize people want a "home away from home" or a "third place" if you will, but just because we know your order doesn't mean that we like you (just kidding).

There is a young lady who comes in, asks for her mocha extra extra sweet, and then, when we make it as she prescribes, comes back and complains that it is "too damn sweet" and she can't drink it. When we ask her if we can make it again, she just wants her money back so she can go to the store she always goes to where they make it right, although it should be noted that she is a regular at our store. Some people literally thrive on being difficult.

Then there is the cute funny man who tells me every day that he likes my hat. He looks uncannily like Wilfred Brimley, although I've heard he gets mad when you mention it.

There are the people who act as though when you mess up their order once in a while that they expect it of you and give you this "smarter-than-thou" look that reads "How are you going to mess up today?" I laugh at these people because I'd like to see them remember 10 people's names and drinks off the top of their head. When I forget that they get two, not three, sugars in their skim milk half-caff latté, for instance, it's probably because I'm a bit frazzled already.

I've always thought it curious that when I'm ringing people up for their order they are very anxious to hand over their money. Often, if they order a pastry along with their coffee, I'll just step over to get it, as the pastry case is right next to the register. I'll see them holding their five-dollar bill out the whole time, even though they can plainly see what I am doing.

There are the people who ask for a small/medium/large "fresh brewed coffee" as the menu board reads. It's just funny because I always want to answer to them, "Oh, you want the FRESH coffee," as if they thought that if they didn't specify we'd give them the three-week-old coffee we keep somewhere in the back.

Speaking of signs, people are so "sign-bound" it's almost pathetic. It's not uncommon for pastry signs to get mixed up and the wrong signs to get put on the wrong thing. I always find it incredible if, say, a "chocolate muffin" sign were accidentally put on, perhaps, a blueberry scone (or something less resembling said chocolate muffin), people (often our regular customers) will go ahead and ask for the chocolate muffin (while meaning the scone, of course). I am always incredulous to this because these are people who see our blueberry scones on a consistent basis, and have no doubt partaken of a blueberry scone once or twice in their day.

While we're on the subject of signs, I don't know if reading is considered too work-related for people to do on their break or if they just can't. When asking for a pastry, they'll just point and say, "That one." It's almost as if they are defiantly refusing to read the sign to tell me what it is. So I have to go to the extra trouble of looking and trying to figure out what the hell they're talking about. Sometimes when they see that I'm not sure which they're pointing to, they'll throw me a line like, "The low-fat one," which only eliminates about half of our selection. You have no idea how aggravating this is. Why can't they just read to me what kind of muffin they want?

I can't stand it when I haven't even finished with a customer and the next customer in line is already handing me his money and making his order. At least give me the courtesy of acknowledging you first.

The people who will ask you a question about something before you can get a word out edgewise are already on a third question in the same line of questioning or are trying to "guess" your answer. Why did they ask me if they are not interested in my answer? Likewise, I can't stand it when people won't even let me finish my question before they start to answer. They're usually not even answering my initial question, which causes tremendous aggravation and time wasted.

It goes something like this:

"How do you like the new muffins?"
"Th…"
"You don't, do you? What about the scones?"
"They…"
"They look really dry. Are they?"
"Not…"
"How's the Sumatra? It's bold, isn't it?"
"It…"
"Are you guys open on Columbus Day?"

You get the idea.

Why do we feel that when we are talking to a member of the opposite sex we must throw in something about "my boyfriend" or "my girlfriend" respectively? I can understand that if the person is unabashedly flirting with you, you may feel it appropriate to boyfriend/girlfriend/drop, but why do we do it in everyday casual conversation?

I always find it amusing when people order "French vanilla" in their beverage. Now there really is a legitimate French vanilla, which consists of vanilla and hazelnut, but the majority of people who order French vanilla in their coffee don't realize that. They are just ordering it because it sounds fancy. Pretentious people are so funny. I'm allowed to say that because I am one as well.

People I don't even know will tell me personal things that are none of my business. There is a lady who comes in occasionally who I can count on one hand the times I have waited on her. The only reason I remember her at all is that, every time, she finds some way to bring up her past anorexia. Something I have had to learn firsthand is that people I don't know are not particularly interested in my psychoses no matter how "OK" I am with them. This is something that she needs to hear. I mean, how does she expect us to follow her "anorexia-related statements?"

"That's greeaaat?"

The people who say that they don't want any room for cream and when they happen to have a mere quarter of a millimeter between the coffee and the rim of the cup, come back complaining that they had specified "No room."

Conversely, I see the people who ask for their coffee black dumping half of it down the trash can in order to put cream in it, or coming back to ask if they could have a "little room for cream." Apparently, as with the fresh coffee, some feel they must differentiate between the black coffee and the purple coffee we sell.

Marcus was an employee of the record store that housed one of the Cafés I worked at. He was also adept at working at the Café, and he filled in when we needed a break or a shift covered. He was quite knowledgeable about the Café, obviously, but he cracked me up because one time I saw him pre-preparing espresso shots and setting them aside. When I asked him what he was doing, he simply said, "I get nervous." I so pity the folks who were the recipients of the drinks with those pre-prepared shots that may have been sitting there for as much as fifteen minutes (an espresso shot shouldn't sit without milk for more than 30 seconds). Needless to say, his services are no longer required at the Café.

Lines

Lines are an interesting phenomenon to some, at least. The Café has three registers. In the early morning hours, we have only one register open. It always amazes me when a customer comes in, sees the long line at the only open register, and trots on over to one of the vacant registers expecting to get served faster there.

Also, they will all line up at the register closest to the door, while they can plainly see that there are two available registers closer in. It might not be so bad, but these are people who come in everyday and are familiar with the way we do deployment.

Brainstem Alert

Jorge is a suave-looking banking executive. His standard order is a large mild coffee with hazelnut, filled to the rim. If we fill it a micro-millimeter beneath the rim, he returns it before you can say "Thank you," reminding you that he wants NO ROOM.

Now that we know his order, this is not a problem except, for one day, I happened to run out of decaf after only filling his cup three quarters of the way. I brought him his decaf with a significant amount (to him, anyway) of space at the top, explaining what had happened. "I don't want any room," he interrupts. "I know that, but the problem is, that we ran out of decaf before I..." I was getting ready to explain to him his options when he said, "You know I'm really getting sick of this. This is becoming a big problem."

Yeah, it's a real bitch when you have to put up with missing an inch of coffee that is only going to end up as backwash.

There was a funny little man who came in who asked for simply a "French vanilla." I took that to mean coffee with French vanilla syrup in it. When he got his beverage, he made it very clear that this was not what he ordered. "I said FRENCH vanilla," as if that were supposed to have made some sort of difference in the way the coffee looked. I

43

explained to him that it was, indeed, a French vanilla coffee. "NO! NO! NO! There is supposed to be whipped cream on this."

Apparently he was meaning to order a vanilla "cappuccino," à la your local minimart, and we ignorant baristas just weren't getting it.

Melanie, who has a terrific way of putting people like that in their place while sounding incredibly sweet, said, "Are you talking about the cappuccinos that you get in gas stations? Because we don't make them like that here." By determining what he wanted, she made him a vanilla latté, which he probably liked more than said cappuccino. Of course, he was too embarrassed to appreciate it. Ignorance is perfectly excusable, but talking down to us when you don't know what the hell you are talking about is very rude, not to mention comical.

I always feel kind of funny when I am trying to remember an order to relay to the barista and I try to clarify if they wanted skim. I often feel like I am being offensive, as if just the fact that I was to imply that they might want skim milk equates to them needing it. This would be preposterous if they did think this because I do the same thing with decaf, which, if you're using the logic that I am trying to influence you (not that I have a horrible memory and don't have time to screw up your order), could possibly equate to "You are so hopelessly boring. You really need something to perk you up." or "Whoa! You are much too hyper. I think we'd better do decaf."

We have two condiment tables (with cream, sugar, napkins, and such). It never fails (I have kept careful track of this) that the one I am (or anyone else is) trying to tidy is the one everyone comes to. Now, my magnetic personality notwithstanding, I just don't understand why, when people see me taking up more than my ordinary share of space (wiping, restocking, changing trash and whatnot), what in the world would possess them to come to that particular condiment bar when they know that the other one has exactly the same assortment of accessories and has much more room!

Joe is someone who is constantly sharing his negative opinion of others to you and, while it is mildly humorous, you just know he's saying similar things about you to other co-workers. Joe is gay and, while not particularly effeminate, his cattiness gives him away. He fancies himself a tolerant liberal, but if you don't think like him he will verbally rip you to shreds. He is very good at his job as an assistant manager, but when he is questioned about anything he is immediately defensive.

François is a pastry chef at the new bakery a few doors down from the Café. Anyone within earshot knows this because he never fails to bring it up in any conversation. His order: an extra-large SIX-SUGAR latté. Eyebrows never fail to rise whenever he makes his order. His response? "I'm a pastry chef. I love sugar." I would imagine he also loves tooth decay.

Nancy is a quiet, very proper lady who I would imagine is in her early fifties. She is the last person anyone would ever suspect of shoplifting. One day I was sitting in the comfortable chair by the door on my lunch break. I was reading, so I was oblivious to what was going on around me until I saw Alan running out the door. Apparently, I found out after the fact that he was (unsuccessfully) chasing Nancy, who had taken a mug off the retail wall.

The next day, Nancy comes in again (???!!!) and is confronted by Alan. She blows it off as a lack of caffeine. I heard that she told someone else, "They forgot to ring me up for this."

Ned is a cute elderly little man who for the longest time I never heard him say anything more than his order (small coffee), until one time when I was tidying up the condiment bar that he was at. He leans over and says, in his usual quiet manner, "Look at all these damn yuppies. I just hate them." It was just so random and unexpected from cute, wouldn't-hurt-a-fly Ned. I think I was laughing the rest of the week over that.

Now there's nothing I find funnier than people having an unexpected secret vice (i.e. the sweet grandmother who secretly is a kleptomaniac) as long as they keep their vagaries in check. For instance, I don't want Ned to come in one day with a semi-automatic rifle and start shooting all the "damn yuppies" (especially since most of them seem to hang out in the Café). In addition, while Nancy's behavior is laughable, stealing is a crime, mind you.

One day Mike was training Stewart at "bussing," i.e. getting the orders for the cashier. It was an unusually busy day, which may have contributed to the stress, but he was taking it out on poor Stew. Stewart, in Mike's eyes, could do nothing right. If Stewart was brewing coffee, he should have been checking condiment stations. If Stewart was checking condiment stations, he shouldn't leave the cashiers in a lurch, making them get their own coffee. Whatever he did, it seemed, was the wrong thing. I saw that Stew was getting a large order, so I started to get the next guy's medium coffee. This, also, was not acceptable to Mike.

Now perhaps this is some sort of "tough-love training" that Mike and Alan are so fond of, but it rarely ever works. I, for one, just get more obstinate and determined not to do it "their way." Other common responses to this type of training are just to give up and walk out or quit shortly after.

Blaine is a fellow barista who is also a dancer. As such, he's the perfect dancer stereotype: fabulously gay and very flamboyant, as one would expect. He is very open about his opinions and his relationships, (or how hot that guy who just came in is), as if anyone cares to know. He is fun to work with, though. He is all pizzazz and "jazz hands," which is kind of fun.

CASE STUDY

Jerry is a super-nice guy but has an annoying habit of always trying to make small talk when he can obviously see that I am otherwise occupied. When I am frantically looking for the milk pitcher, he asks me who left the cup of water on the side of the bar or something similarly trivial.

It may be that when he sees any of us looking at all intense, he wants to (in his mind only) try to make it better to a) attempt to lighten the mood [again, in his mind only], and b) to sort of make sure he is not the reason for our intensity, which is counterproductive because we do end up being short or impatient with him.

Similarly, why do people, when they can plainly see I have a million things on my mind, choose that precise moment to ask me questions like, "How was your weekend?" or anything that makes me take my mind off of the situation at hand?

Now, don't get me wrong, I know these people are just being friendly and I am not trying to discourage it because Lord knows there is enough animosity in the world (and the Café). It is neither nice nor friendly when you can see that we are struggling to juggle five things and then you throw us something else.

Now if this isn't the pot calling the kettle black, I don't know what is. I know how annoying this is, and yet what is the first thing I do when I go into our local deli? I try to carry on a conversation with the owner/manager John who works there and is slammed up to his eyeballs with sandwich orders. This, of course, is different. The point is - we all do it.

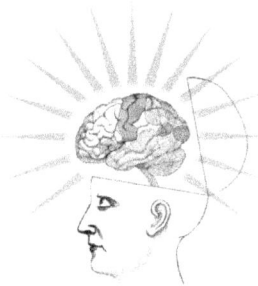

Brainstem Alert

Diana Diamond is a local newscaster in our area. A lot of the TV folks patron the Café, so it's not uncommon to see any of them at any time during the week. Most of them are very nice. This one particular day, though, was a different story. I almost immediately recognized Diana and said something like, "Oh! You're on the news!" To which she smiled and nodded her head. "What can I get for you?" I asked. "A medium coffee," she responded. I reached to grab the cup and was having trouble separating it from the plastic wrap which covered the whole stack of cups. Since it was taking a few extra minutes, I did what I would always do in this situation: make small talk with the customer. "So are you still doing mostly 5:30 newscasts?"

Her answer was more than a little curt. "Look, I have to be on the air in 15 minutes." I hand her the coffee and she hustles out the door.

Now, in my reptilian mode, I was glad that I could give Ms. Diamond the apparent "acclaim" she was lacking. To be fair, it's probably not uncommon for busy Café workers to waste precious time fawning over small-game newscasters, and she was, after all running late. I'm sure the gourmet coffee cup in hand went over well back at the station. I can picture it now: "I'm so sorry, but I simply had to get my cappuccino, and well, you know how the fans are…"

Now, this is a prime example of a "brainstem alert." Diana was stressed because she was in a hurry. In her reptilian state, she was not too concerned with manners. Since I didn't know about the reptilian brain at the time, I just thought she was an uppity bitch.

The reptilian brain has no concept of good or evil. It just acts. It doesn't know the difference between productive or destructive action. That is how we can go back and forth between animosity and peacefulness. It is human nature at its basest, most depraved state, except for the fact that we are, in actuality, reptiles.

I have learned, mostly through experience, that most negative or aggressive reactions have little to do with the unfortunate soul who happens to be the target. Often they are the product of a false "first impression," or maybe a previous experience, which doesn't have anything to do with the person being vented upon, or even the situation at hand. The brain will often hold fast to these initial impressions, especially in times of stress. The result can be, and is often, varying degrees of aggression.

Now please don't misunderstand, I am not in any way excusing Diana's (or anyone's) negative brainstem behavior. Indeed, we have just learned about the tenacity of the reptilian brain. It is very hard to overcome, and it may seem impossible at times.

CASE STUDY

Karen is one of my favorite superiors to work with. The only thing is, whenever I express discontent, be it with her personally or how I feel about the new policy Alan is implementing, she always comments on how "mean" I am. ("Uh oh! Brooke's pissed!") I am a fairly easygoing person, so in her eyes if I am not being the happy/nice person I usually am, I'm apparently, in her eyes, being mean. This also bothers me when anyone does it. Just because I am in a relatively good mood most of the time does that exempt me from anger or frustration? Why is it if I don't have a smile on my face that I am assumed to be upset?

CASE STUDY

The Café has four airpots of coffee: one regular, one decaf. We also have a back-up pot of each. There is a foreign man who regularly patrons the Café who is referred to simply as "back-pot" man. This is because he always requests coffee from the back pot, even though I have explained to him on more than one occasion that if I were supposed to be serving from the back pot it would be in the front and referred to as such. More often than not, we don't even have a back pot, as we haven't had a need to brew it yet.

Why back-pot man feels he is privy to the back pot, while everyone else has to wait, is beyond me. I'm not sure if this is brainstem-related or just arrogance.

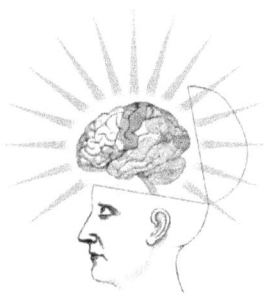

Brainstem Alert

Marla is a Café worker who seems to have a dual personality. On the one hand, she can be incredibly laid back, with a relaxed attitude. On the other hand, she can be way uptight and priggishly by the book on everything. She tends to vacillate between the two. When Marla's relaxed, she's fun and cool, but when she's stressed, she's anything but.

This confusing behavior of Marla's stems from her own control issues. She has a basic need to be in control, though she probably doesn't even realize it. As long as she feels in control, she can be relaxed, but the moment she feels the situation is a trifle out of her hands, the reptile in her brain comes out and she goes back to the one thing she knows won't let her down. Ordinarily she seems a bit "fly by the seat of her pants" impulsive. So when she makes the switch, people are understandably very confused.

CASE STUDY

David is a recent graduate of the local university. He is charming and hard-working. The Café is obviously not his first choice of a place to work. He is quite talkative and spends any available time schmoozing with the businessmen trying to make connections for a better job. He is also quite girl-crazy. When he is not schmoozing with the businessmen, he is schmoozing with the ladies. Up until recently, he has been unsuccessful at both.

Poor David. He is actually quite the catch. He just tries too hard. He is a very likable fellow, although he really wore on everyone's nerves when he was at the Café. I think the reason we found him annoying was that he epitomized everyone's worst fears about themselves.

EVERYONE would have rather been working somewhere else. EVERYONE had someone that they would be interested in pursuing romantically. I think that they just hoped that they wouldn't pursue either to the extent that David seemed to.

I know that I personally tend to not like people who remind me of myself. I think that it's safe to say that it is true to some extent for most others as well. People tend not to like people who remind them of what they don't like about themselves. It's sort of like watching a tape of the time you tripped and fell in front of the hundreds of people at the school pep rally a hundred times over.

David's efforts did eventually pay off. Last I heard he landed a corporate job, just as he had hoped. Perhaps he landed himself a lady as well.

Corporations Are Strange

While Corporate will go out of their way to accommodate offenses, they will still allow an Alanis Morissette song that is very offensive to Catholics and Christians alike (a huge client base, by the way) to be played on their in-store music compilations. It just seems like a huge double standard.

I have never been "on board" with the whole "politically correct" movement. Unfortunately, Corporate feels they must be. (and perhaps they do, after all, you don't want to alienate your customers). But this, like anything else can be taken too far. You're always going to step on toes. You just kind of have to pick and choose who's toes you want to step on. That, or you just end up sounding ridiculously generic.

One Christmas I was wishing people I knew to be Christians a Merry Christmas when Alice told me that I needed to say "Happy Holidays" because they may not celebrate Christmas. If I were in Jerusalem, I would think nothing of someone wishing me Happy Hanukkah. I wouldn't be offended, or feel the need to explain that "I don't celebrate Hanukkah. I'm Christian." Why can't we just let well wishes be well wishes?

I had a cute little pin that had the chemical notation of decaf coffee with a slash through it. I wore it the whole morning until Alice told me to take it off because when you wear things that imply taking a stand for something, people take it the wrong way.

We had a popular seasonal drink with very popular syrup. It was no longer being offered, and customers were upset. Most stores had a way to concoct it with the existing syrups. One evening, I went into the store I frequent when I'm not working. I requested the concoction version. The barista that evening was a friend and told me that he'd make it for me, but he had been told by his manager that he wasn't allowed to make it anymore because they were supposed to be plugging their new seasonal drinks.

CASE STUDY

DeMarcus is a custodial employee for the mall that houses the Café. He usually stopped in for a morning coffee before his shift. He had a habit of referring to the ladies as "Sweetie." Now this was more than likely something he (or any of the other millions of people who do it) ever thought twice about, but he said it to the wrong person when he said it to Melissa.

In Melissa's words, "It's just too familiar. I don't know him." She let it go on for several months before she decided to say something to him. Since she figured he may not know her name, she said one day; "My name is Melissa. I prefer that to 'Sweetie.'" He came in one more time after that to ask if she was mad at him, which she assured him that she wasn't. But, alas, he never came back.

Now maybe Melissa is just too sensitive and shouldn't have said anything. After all, DeMarcus was just trying to be nice and didn't mean anything by it. But I see it another way. Yes, it was just DeMarcus's way of being friendly, but if it made Melissa uncomfortable, I think she was fully in her right to say something. I don't think people realize that it is very degrading, not to mention condescending, to some waitresses to be called "sweetie," "honey," or "baby" by men we don't even know, nor care to. It's even worse if a woman does it because it comes across as waaaay more condescending.

I've actually discovered that people, whether consciously or unconsciously, use terms of condescension like that when they are feeling insecure about themselves. It's a way to bring the other person down to their level, but I think for the most part the person saying it doesn't realize it.

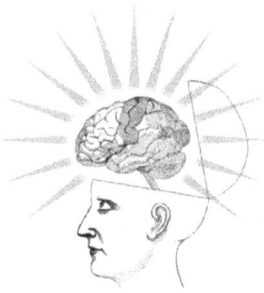

Brainstem Alert

Tanisha was eavesdropping on a conversation that Billy and Meagan were having regarding rapper Kanye West's slandering of President Bush.

"…I used to like Kanye until he made that comment about Bush," Billy was telling Meagan. Meagan was nodding her head, but before she could respond, Tanisha interrupted, with indignation.

"Why shouldn't he have said that? He's right! George Bush is a murderer."

"I hear he also hates black people," Meagan said sarcastically.

"Damn straight he hates black people. When the tsunami hit, we were right there, but New Orleans had to wait two weeks before he sent aid." (Tanisha was getting louder and louder with every accusatory statement & the customers were looking quite uncomfortable.)

Now the fact that Tanisha has no idea what she's talking about aside, as she just parrots the latest liberal "groupthink," work is no place for politics, especially as loud as she was being.

I am completely guilty of this as well, but at least I try not to be so loud and emotional about it. But it is just as wrong, even though I do enjoy ruffling people's feathers, which is also wrong. I am making my confession so as to not be calling the kettle black.

I have a horrible memory, so I am forever writing notes to myself which sometimes, if I don't have a pocket, I'll just leave in a neat stack by my register. Alan, being the neatnik that he is, is constantly throwing away my notes, assuming that they are trash. Now this doesn't sound bad in and of itself, but I just can't stand it when people hover over me. I wonder how he would feel if I just threw away stuff that I perceived to be trash on his desk.

One time I confronted Alan about his "hovering" and micromanaging, which probably in some universe is an effective management style; however, in our present galaxy it is both unproductive and annoying. He, however, didn't see it my way and immediately got defensive. "I'm not going to apologize for doing my job."

Charmeka is borrowing money from the tip jar yet again. Alan overhears Charmeka and Beth planning their monthly breakfast outing for Saturday. "You know, I find it interesting that you have money for breakfast but have to borrow money for lunch." He then goes on a 15- to 20-minute lecture about responsibility with money. After Charmeka is out of earshot, he says to Beth, "I guess it's pointless to try to tell her how to live her life." It's a good thing that isn't his job, though. From the way he talks, you'd think it was. While Alan may be right, Charmeka did not ask his opinion on anything.

Another curious thing about Alan is he will be such a stickler for certain sanitation principles yet overlook seemingly obvious ones. For instance, he will have me wash my hands after I sneeze (in my arms, so as to avoid contaminating my hands), yet he will allow the gloves with which we handle food to reside in the dirty drawer where we keep the pastry signs, which are not too terribly clean. And speaking of pastry signs, we have the kind that clip onto the trays. That's a good idea in and of itself, yet the dirty clips usually end up touching the food. It's just stuff like that you would think the manager of a Café would be more mindful of.

Personal Space:
Why you gotta be all up in my GRILL?

Hope is a very touchy-feely sort. You know the type: someone who always has to find some way to touch you to emphasize a point. Hope would be bussing, and I would be on register. She would be asking what she could get for a customer, all the while draping her arm all over me. Well, the combination of the small space, the broken air conditioning, and just the pure annoyance of it got to me. I finally snapped.

"OK, it is much too hot in here for that." I felt bad, so when the line had died down, I apologized, explaining how I needed my space. Apparently, that was all that needed to be done because she backed off after that. Even better, I noticed other co-workers making a concentrated effort to steer clear as well.

Personal space is a curious thing. Some people are more protective of it than others. Me, I need lots of it; I'm very claustrophobic. I would love to do a study on what causes the great divide between those who need space and those who don't because neither understands the other, and their phobias and impulses play off of each other so distinctly.

Unfortunately, annoyance is all too common at the Café. It is in these situations that it seems our brainstems have taken over our bodies. It is not uncommon, however, for orders to be repeated. There is always a lot going on, so often it will slip by unnoticed by the cashiers that the people who are bussing or on the espresso bar have already received a specific order.

"I already HAVE that," is the reptilian reply uttered by Alan and Mike.

I realize that Alan and Mike, being in authority roles, are probably the most stressed out and therefore always dealing with reptilian brain, both of their own and others. They probably don't realize, or don't care, that we more often than not "catch" their reptile, so to speak. If they were able to reason, they would realize that most people are not just talking to hear themselves talk. I don't just shout out orders because I enjoy it. The interesting thing is that if someone neglects to relay an order to them, they are in even deeper shit.

Another common misunderstanding I've encountered in the same situation is that when I'm repeating an order back to the customer to clarify that I have it right, the busser will often overhear and assume that I am calling it to them. This is common & usually not a problem, except for when Mike is bussing. I'll call out a medium mild. He will ask, "Is that the same medium mild you just called out?" Then I will say, "I didn't call out a medium mild." To which he will responds (in fight mode) very adamantly, "Yes you did."

Now I can understand how he might overhear something and think either I was calling it, or about to call it, and if it were anyone else perhaps I wouldn't be as upset. I just know that if the situation were reversed it would be me who was in the wrong. It is always a double standard with Mike.

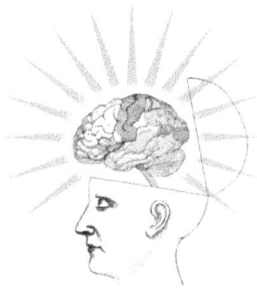

Brainstem Alert

LaTonya is very quick with the drinks on the espresso bar. She can usually handle the massive rushes we tend to get in the mornings. The only thing is that she does little to control her reptilian brain. We usually have quite a few orders back to back. Before long, she starts to take her frustrations out on the people relaying the orders to her.

"Order."
"Yes, Hope," with a tone oozing with sarcasm and disdain.

After a while, it just gets to you, as being treated constantly and consistently with disrespect will do. Again, Hope is not talking just to hear the sound of her own voice. It's not respectful to Hope or, more importantly, the customer.

One day a water main broke on one of the major streets in town. This unfortunately left the whole city, along with the Café, without any water for about an hour. Yet even so, people were still coming to the Café to get their coffee and espresso drinks, neither of which we've managed to figure out how to make without water. Even with this oversight aside, the customers' incredulous responses may have been mildly humorous the first time we heard it:"WHAT??!! NO COFFEE? A CAFÉ WITHOUT COFFEE?"

For one thing, it's the same people who say that in every such instance; furthermore, when you've heard it 100 times in the past 30 minutes, it's just not funny.

Tom, Ernie, and Fred are three investment brokers who come in everyday. While I do have an enormous amount of orders stored in my brain, for some reason theirs aren't one of them, probably because they don't say anything more to me to make me want to remember it. One day, after placing their orders, Fred says to me, "You know, we have a bet going as to when you're going to remember our orders." Unfortunately, he hasn't sped up the process any.

This seemingly innocent comment was counterproductive for a couple of reasons. First, I don't know why I remember the specific names and orders I do, but it does have a lot to do with customer interaction, of which I've had little to none with any of them. Second, expecting me to remember your order and verbalizing this expectation to me puts me on the defensive (thus provoking the reptile in my brain). You shouldn't expect me to remember your order out of the millions I take every hour. These guys, hell, they can't even remember my name, which is a lot simpler than their three orders. In these sorts of situations, I don't want to. In fact, I am doing everything in my power to forget their orders.

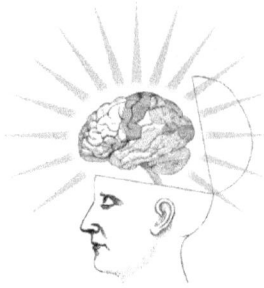

Brainstem Alert

One day I had accidentally made too much "ready-to-brew" decaf. I hadn't measured it before grinding the whole bag of coffee, which was my oversight, and I admitted it. Mike, acting supervisor that day, got all over me during the middle of a line going out the door. He kept hammering questions at me like, "Is there any reason you made this much decaf? Because you know we're just going to end up throwing it away. See all the coffee you've wasted?"

While he had asked for my reasoning he obviously wasn't interested in my answer, which he said as much when I interjected. I finally interjected, "Are you going to let me talk?" He shot back with a very sarcastic "I really want to hear your answer."

Mike was in brainstem mode because he knew that he would be yelled at for my oversight. While I was sympathetic to his brainstem (especially since I had caused it), I didn't want to put up with it. He wasn't able to think rationally, so he took his (deserved) aggression out on me.

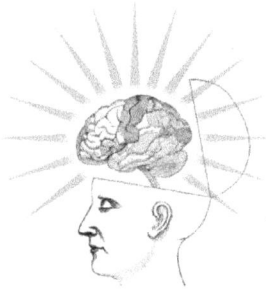

Brainstem Alert

Ted is a high-strung, uptight individual for whom I had the pleasure of briefly working. It always amuses me when uptight people fancy themselves laid back (I can say this because I am one of them). Ted and his wife Sally were opening a coffee shop right about the time I began my interest in the coffee industry. I was working at a neighboring ice cream shop when I met both of them. To make a long story short, I quit my higher-paying job at the ice cream shop to work for them. A week or so later, they decided my schedule was much too restrictive, and they laid me off.

"Nothing personal. It's just business," Sally told me.

I called her back when I later had time to process and ask questions about why I was being laid off, and Ted answered. He wouldn't talk to me. "I just can't talk about this," he said with the pitch of his voice rising into a panic.

This is an example of the "flight" alternative of brainstem thinking. Ted wanted away from me because I was a stressful situation.

The Café, being a starting minimum wage, food service establishment, tends to attract employees from all walks of life. At the time, it was the unschooled, non-professional people with whom I was able to group myself (lest you think I'm judging). In fact, while by no means am I being all inclusive, the majority of the management is of this ilk. It is very interesting how they treat the subordinates, especially the ones who are in school; it is almost as if they are trying to tear down in order to build themselves up.

Few things enrage me more than people I hardly speak to thinking that they know anything about me. I may only choose to divulge a certain aspect of my life to these people, namely customers. When people ask what I did over the weekend, as they usually do, I either can't remember or don't care to share details because I either don't think it's any of their business, or I don't have the time to go into it right then. My catchall answer is usually "nothin'." (In middle school that was all the cool people did... "nothin'"). Of course, that is not always a true statement. Sometimes it is, but more often than not it means, "I don't have the time to tell you." So it really pisses me off when Joe Banker, who I don't even recognize, comes in on a Monday and says "So, did you have your usual non-eventful weekend?" I don't like it from anyone who comes in the Café since no one knows me well enough to say that to me, but it bordered on amusing when someone I didn't even know said it to me. I know a lot of it is that I simply take things too personally, but seriously, it takes a LOT of nerve to assume you know anything about me when I don't even know who you are.

In the same vein, there is an older man who is just way too familiar with us. He "insults" us, but he means it in a friendly way. The thing is, I don't know him well enough for that. He hasn't earned that right from me. For instance, he told me one time, when I happened to be sick, "You look like you just got up." I merely said "Thank you," and moved on.

A lot of people at the Café know my name before I know theirs. For a long time, it used to be a huge pet peeve of mine to address me by my name before we had formally met. I thought it presumptuous and familiar (plus I would go crazy trying to think of their name and how it was that I knew them). Oh how I wished that I could take the attitude of my friend, Tabitha, who says, "It makes me feel famous when people know who I am." I am finally there, but for the longest time, it just annoyed me.

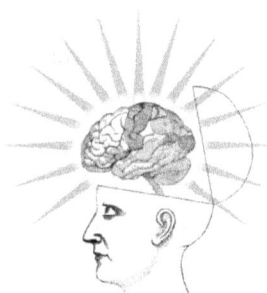

Brainstem Alert

Becky and Mike were opening the Café one day. Since the scheduled time to arrive when opening is 5:00am, it is not uncommon for people to oversleep (i.e. alarm clock malfunctions and snooze buttons). Becky, an everyday opener, is very understanding if her supervisor happens to be late. "It happens," she says. It could just as easily happen to me.

Becky arrived at the store at 5:00. Mike apparently had overslept and did not arrive until 5:45. The store opens at 6:00am. Rushing to open the Café frazzled Becky a little, but she wasn't too upset until Mike demanded to know why the extra coffee hadn't been weighed using the new method described to Becky just two days ago.

So, apparently, when a supervisor is late, the one who got there on time isn't allowed to be a bit out of sorts when the pressure is on to perform all of the opening duties in 10 frazzled minutes. In addition, they are also supposed to remember recent minor changes to the routine that has remained constant for years.

James is a recent high school graduate whose youthful appearance and childish manner might ordinarily be considered endearing if it weren't so darn annoying. His insecurity about himself is fairly obvious. The way he copes with it is downright laughable. He really isn't the brightest bulb in the chandelier, but that is probably because of his age; you're allowed to be stupid at 20. The annoying thing is, whenever he is informed of *anything* that he didn't already know, be it the quantum physics String Theory concept, to the location of a certain bar, he would turn the tables on you and act as though you were stupid for expecting him to know the information.

For example, one time James happened to mention that he got more of a "jolt" from a shot of espresso than from coffee, to which I told him that espresso actually had less caffeine than coffee. He argumentatively denied this up and down for the next five minutes or so until the other baristas all concurred that espresso did, in fact, have less. When he finally saw he was outnumbered, and that we were being perfectly serious and probably knew more about it than he did, he went on a condescending rant.

"Well, I'm no gourmet coffee *connoisseur*, or whatever. I mean, I have other things to fill my knowledge with…."

Sadly, you would think that this is a rare occurrence; unfortunately it is not. It is amazing how defensive grown men and women will get if they feel they are being "challenged" on something they really don't need to know.

On the other hand, you have the people, well-meaning as they are, who try to find out about the inner workings of the Café and then act like they are so smart because now have the "inside track." If we happen to change procedures, as we often do, they act all chagrinned that we aren't doing it the right way.

Mark is an older gentleman who is very nice but borders on being too familiar. He is not alone in his vice. He suffers from the "I-know-it-all-even-though-I-don't-know-any-of-the-details" syndrome. He knew Martine was about to graduate from college and just assumed she was looking for a job. He asked her how her job hunt was going. Martine has a lot on her plate and is making decent money at the Café, so she is not really looking for a job right now. Not wishing to divulge details, she simply told him she wasn't looking.

"O-kay." He said in a tone that may as well have said "These kids today don't know what the hell they're doing."

Now, granted, Mark was just trying to be pleasant making conversation, showing that he remembered something about her, but he was acting way too familiar and making judgments about things he knew nothing about.

On the other side of the coin, I realize some people, myself included, can be way too judgmental about things like this. Everyone has a story and corresponding reasons for why they act the way they do that we don't always know or understand.

I am reminded of an old episode of *The Walton's* where prim "oh-so-smarter-than-thou" Cora-Beth had just been informed by Jim Bob what he and the rest of the town thought of her. In essence, her response was that when she was young she had always dreamed of being a ballerina and an actress but couldn't afford to pursue either career. So here she was, a shopkeeper's wife on Walton's Mountain, which was a far cry from the hubbub of New York. Ballet or dramatic productions were limited to the glamour of school and church plays. So she read good literature and spoke with correct grammar as a way of realizing her dream.

Remember the game of "gossip" we used to play in kindergarten? You know, when the whole class would sit in a circle and someone would say a sentence and each person would whisper said phrase into the ear of the person next to them and by the time it got back to the author, it was so badly massacred that it was something entirely different? For instance what started out as "I like the color red," and by the time it went around the circle it became something like, "I want you dead."

One day a movie was being filmed across the street from the Café. This, of course, drew a crowd of onlookers. No one really knew what was going on. It had been rumored that Will Ferrell would be filming a movie in town, so everyone thought that this might be it. Then I heard something about the Olsen twins. It was just funny how many different speculations I heard put forth as truth. I did find out the next day that one of my co-workers saw Kate Hudson.

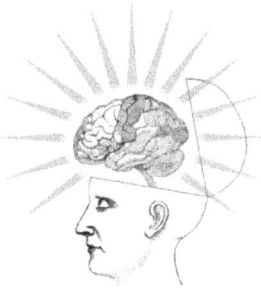

Brainstem Alert

One morning, George, it seemed, had overslept. George had not been feeling well the day prior.

"George is late," Michelle commented disparagingly.

"Maybe he overslept. He is sick, you know," Lana pointed out.

"Or maybe he just didn't want to come in today," Michelle said.

"Isn't LaTonya covering his shift?" Lana asked

"No, because she is closing tonight. He will probably use that as an excuse because he didn't want to work today. He was trying to find someone yesterday to cover his shift."

I just love how everyone expects the worst at the Café. Now poor George wasn't even there to defend himself. He did show up a few minutes late. He looked like hell warmed over, he was so sick.

Assuming the worst about people seems to be the common motif at the Café, with managers anyway. I don't know why they haven't realized doing that is not at all productive and does little for employee morale.

I've always found it fascinating how the slightest change in routine can completely throw people off. For instance, we ran out of small cups, so when someone ordered a small drink, we would put the smaller size in a medium cup.

This posed all sorts of problems. People were either extremely confused (you know, the kind of deep perplexity that you can just read all over a face) or wouldn't realize it was a larger cup until they saw how much lower than usual from the rim that it was, and they would come back complaining that we had gypped them and demand more coffee. I am such a creature of routine, but I'd like to think that even I roll with the punches a lot easier than the majority of these folks.

Speaking of changes in routine, I am such a creature of habit it's a wonder I try anything new. One day I was working at another Café (the Café has other locations), which of course had its own differences, with the main one being that when you rang up an order in the cash register it would then relay the order to the espresso bar on a separate monitor above the bar. This was very different from our store because we had to do it the old-fashioned way: we simply yelled the order out to the barista. I was manning the espresso bar when I got so wrapped up in a couple of orders that I forgot to push "next" on the monitor, which would then delete the handed-off order and display the rest of the orders.

I was growing more confused by the minute. *Why didn't they call this one?* I would wonder. The line started growing with people anxious for their beverages. Long story short: that store is still talking about what a loser I am.

I find it quite intriguing in our conversations that the majority of the time we barely even know what the other person is saying because we are so concerned with what we are going to say next. I keep meaning to try saying something completely outrageous to someone I know isn't paying attention, just for fun.

A lady came in on her lunch break and bought several glass items: mugs, saucers, etc. which needed to be wrapped in tissue paper. I couldn't locate the tissue paper, which was not where it was usually kept. After going around trying to locate it, all the while asking several co-workers, I was told it was in the closet, which is in the men's bathroom. I went to said closet and looked all over. I found a box which could possibly have housed the MIA tissue paper, but it was so lodged in an extremely high shelf that getting it out was no easy feat. Not wanting to take up any more of this poor woman's time, I asked my manager to check to see if it was indeed what I was looking for and to try to get it out so that I could assist her with the rest of her order.

When Alan finally retrieved the box, which was indeed the tissue paper, he brought it to me with a "Here, Brooke" that plainly said he had misunderstood my whole MO. I never said that I couldn't find it. I never said that there wasn't any tissue paper in the closet.

Can You Hear Me Now?

Can I just say something about cell phones? Yes, they are wonderful inventions; but I am convinced that people in my generation or older who feel they must have them surgically attached to their ear are still secretly enamored with the whole "futuristic" aspect of them (as I am) because, I'm sorry, no one can be that busy. If you are, well then you should be rich enough to send servants or something to run and fetch your coffee. As for the people who are several years my junior, I am convinced they carry them just to feel important.

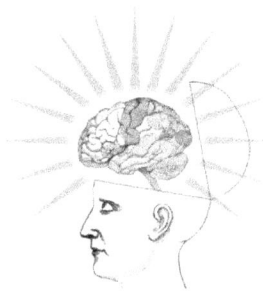

Brainstem Alert

One very busy day in particular a lady I had never seen before came to my register and ordered a medium latté and asked if I could "make it a little darker." Never in all my years of coffee service had I ever heard it put that way. I've heard of adding shots, obviously, but she seemed to know what she was talking about, so I asked her:

"What do you mean by that?"

She may have perceived it as huffy, which certainly was not my intention this time. She was visibly peeved at me, so I explained:

"I'm not really sure what you mean by that. A medium latté comes with two shots; you can add as many as you'd like. Would you like to add a third shot?"

"I'd like just a half a shot extra," she said to me with a tone and a look that clearly said that somehow this should have been obvious and I should have clearly guessed this from the beginning. She was plainly mad at me. I'm not extremely proud that I did stoop to her level and wished her a very sarcastic good day (only a little).

There are several key lessons we can draw from this scenario. One, don't assume I know what you are talking about when you are unsure of it yourself. Two, don't get mad at me if I don't immediately pick up on what it is you want. Three, don't get annoyed when I explain how WE do it here.

I guess an additional lesson for me in this scenario is not to give people the benefit of the doubt that they know what they are talking about. I was actually thinking that maybe this was some new hip way of ordering lattés. Oh well.

This is a prime example of reptile thinking being contagious. In response to her reptilian behavior, I allowed myself to engage in behavior of the same sort. It could have been the other way around if she perceived me being reptilian first. It's easy to play off of each other's reptiles.

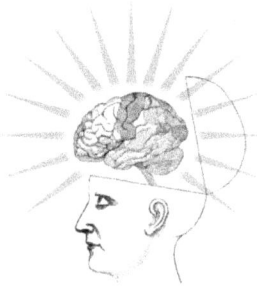

Brainstem Alert

Melinda was on register one particularly busy day. Mike was on bar and really, really stressed, and understandably so. The java jackets (they protect your hand from the cup's heat) are kept under Melinda's register.

Mike had run out of sleeves and apparently didn't have the usual spare basket in place for just such emergencies. He handed the empty basket to Melinda, and when she started to take time away from the customer who she was currently ringing up to fill them up, Mike said, in a very annoyed voice, "I don't have time to wait for you to fill them up." So Melinda stepped even further from her register to grab the almost empty basket that the bussers were using for the drip coffee. "That doesn't help me at all," Mike said.

Why Mike was yelling at Melinda is beyond me. It wasn't even her job to get the basket for him. That was the busser's job.

Reptiles on Caffeine

Misdirected anger is another prevalent problem at the Café. Since you don't have anyone to immediately yell at, you just yell at the first available target. There were several available targets, but Melinda was the one who got hit.

I have had much experience with misdirected anger on both the giving and the receiving end. It's unfortunately unavoidable, but it CAN be somewhat controlled; you just have to want to make a true effort.

Alan, unfortunately, doesn't help matters when (in his brainstem mode) the first thing (before "Hi") he says to me is that I have the wrong shirt on. Or when he's consistently pointing out when I am wrong, like the time I was describing to a customer that sometimes it's as if I'm immune to caffeine (because I need so much more to take effect). Alan piped in with "She can still tell when she needs it, so she can't be immune." Since there are no reasoning skills in the brainstem, hyperbole and descriptive speech are completely lost on him when he's in this state, especially when he's trying to point out my "error." Since the brainstem tends to make us combative, it is good advice to everyone to learn to control their respective reptiles.

I find it fascinating, not to mention unsettling, that much of our aggression stems from how secure we are with ourselves. I know this firsthand because I have employed this method of building myself up more times than I care to admit. When someone is dissatisfied with their work performance, they are more likely to lash out at others. This can be from a variety of reasons, not the least of which is that possibly they feel threatened by them but can also be simply because they need a scapegoat on who they can get away with pinning blame.

77

Double Standards

Alan has a funny quirk. He'll remember if you have a hang-up about something, and then use it against you. For instance, I have a major hang-up about washing my hands after handling something like the trash, the rags we use to wipe the counters or tables, or even the boxes that the pastries are delivered in. I don't know whose dirty hands have been handling them, or what dirty box they've been in. I am apparently (and sadly) the only one who thinks about this.

Kathy, another co-worker, apparently is more sensitive to being disrespectful to people and apologized to Alan because she felt that she had been disrespectful one time to him (she wasn't; she was just disagreeing with him).

With knowledge of these supposed "hang-ups" under his belt, Alan accuses Kathy of being disrespectful whenever she questions or dares to disagree with him. In the same way, he harped on me the ONE time I didn't wash my hands (which was wrong; I'm not denying it).

The point is, he won't say a thing to any of the other workers about these wrongs, which are apparently only wrong when we do them. He and the others are free to serve with dirty hands and be disrespectful.

Since the Café is a food establishment, the employees are all required to wear hats. The corporation which owns the Café makes sun visors that have the logo on it. Some of the employees have started to wear them instead of the standard-issue hats. They are much more comfortable to wear.

However, no one seems to have picked up on the fact that they are not health code. It's like having a hat that you don't have to wear. They don't restrain the hair enough.

Even worse, Maggie, one day, decides to wear her hair out over the visor so it is completely unrestrained. Alan, to my amazement, allows it. And when Maggie asks how it looks, Alan says, "Fine."

Our district manager comes in the same day and sees the hair over the hat. I was sure that would be the end of it. She allowed it as well. I guess I never will get those food establishment rules.

I was bussing for a change and, since I am not perfect like Alan and do make mistakes once in a while, happened to leave the milk carafes out in the serving area instead of taking them to the back as I usually do. Alan, of course, was the first to bring this to my attention.

"We take the carafes to the back to wash," he informs me.
"I know, I usually do that, but must have left them out there by accident."

"I've seen you leave them up front before. Well, I actually I haven't been here to see..."

It was a good thing he stopped when he did or it may have gotten reptilian. For one thing I was under a lot of stress already and was in no mood to defend myself over something that I shouldn't have to. I mean, I know what is true. The problem is Alan doesn't usually let it lie as easily as he just did.

Margaret is a lady of about 45 or so, with a perpetual sour look on her face. I don't believe I've ever seen her smile. She has an unusual order, which, as it turns out, I had been ringing up wrong for several years, to her benefit. When she came in one day and Kristi rang it up properly, it was about $2 dollars more. Of course Margaret understandably complained that the price wasn't correct.

Alan, who was within earshot, explained to Margaret that she had been undercharged all of those other times. This was not what Margaret wanted to hear, so she got a real attitude and stalked out. I can understand how, in her brainstem mode, she probably wasn't thankful to me for all the times I actually saved her money.

I was filling in at another store one day when a lady came to my register and asked for a "refill." She didn't seem to have a cup, so I asked her if someone was already helping her. She said no. At this point I was so confused. "You want a refill, but you don't have a cup?" She replied, "I don't want to deal with this. This is what I ask for everyday." With that she stormed out.

I guess she felt I was challenging her, which I wasn't (This would explain her reptilian fight and flight response). I was more concerned with her getting her coffee, which was why I was concerned about the whereabouts of her cup. If she had just told me that the definition of "refill" was standard at this location, I would have been more than happy to oblige.

It's amazing to me how both Mike and Alan will point out something I did "wrong" in the middle of a rush. For instance, a lot of times they are bussing and will hear an order as the customer is placing it. Most bussers will just get it, or say they have it. I usually call it regardless so that I cannot be accused of not calling an order. Mike rarely hesitates to respond, in a very annoyed tone, that he already has said order. After several of those situations, I will just stop calling him orders I figure he has already heard. In those instances, he will wait a few minutes and then ask "Did you have a medium mild, Brooke?" as a way to teach me, I presume, that at the Café we call out our drinks.

However, if the roles were reversed and he was calling the drinks and I was bussing, I would be wrong because "Everyone is talking clearly and loudly."

Mike and Sandy were opening one Tuesday morning. Sandy was setting up the pastry case. When she got to the cupcakes, she discovered two, one chocolate and one vanilla, which were in one tray without a date on it. Sandy knew that they were probably just left over from yesterday and were still good. Still, the lack of date bothered her, as they looked as though they were to be donated to the local shelter. She also knew that if she had neglected to put a date on an opened pastry, she would never hear the end of it. So she asked Mike, which apparently was a mistake. (So much for being conscientious.)

Mike immediately got huffy and, in a tone that unmistakably said that Sandy should have known better, said, "Well today is Tuesday, so they must have been opened Monday and since they have a two-day shelf life, you can deduce by process of elimination that they are still good."

While this does make complete sense, I have been told repeatedly by Mike himself that no matter what the day is, we need to label because "you really can't play guessing games." Furthermore, he has actually thrown out stuff that I did not label (for the exact reason he was describing—that it was "perfectly obvious").

Alan, as I should know by now, can never be wrong. If you bring something to his attention that he did do wrong, his reptilian brain always has a million different reasons as to why he was right. In other words, it's always the other person's fault. When caught in the headlights, the reptilian brain's main concern is survival.

You know, it's interesting that all of us work different positions at the Café and know what's involved in each respective position (and what annoys us when we are in another position). Unfortunately, it doesn't change how we react to others in other positions. For instance, when I'm working register, I can't stand it when the "bussers" don't acknowledge right away that they have my orders. When I'm bussing, I think that the register people just need to calm down, because, clearly, I AM getting to everyone. It's a total double standard that NO ONE is immune from.

Every shift has a shift supervisor, although, on any given shift, there can be multiple "supervisors." It is often hard to keep up with who is actually running the shift. One extremely busy day in particular,

Tammy had run out of five-dollar bills in her register. Tammy knew that Phylicia was in charge that day. Phylicia seemed to be rather engaged in a conversation with a customer while working the bar during the busy rush. She apparently made the wrong decision when she told Mike. Mike is also a supervisor, and Tammy was hoping that Mike would relay the message to Phylicia, but, as nothing usually turns out as expected at the Café, Mike went ballistic.

"I'm not the shift supervisor. Phylicia is."

"I know, but she seems a bit occupied," Tammy said having just noticed that Mike was rather occupied himself. Of course, by now Phylicia could hear what was going on. Mike was understandably peeved at Tammy's apparent insensitivity but automatically jumped to the wrong conclusion and assumed the worse. This was displayed afterward when Tammy met with both Mike and Phylicia afterward to "clear her name."

Mike's account said that Tammy had asked for more fives, and when Mike said that he wasn't the right person to talk to, Tammy had said, "Well I still need more fives, so..."

This, of course, was preposterous to Tammy, who knew she had made no such response. "I'm pretty sure I didn't say that," she said. Mike had nothing more to say.

It just goes to show how, in a highly stressful situation, we tend to hear what we want to hear and not what is actually being said. Everyone does it. I don't think it's as malicious as it sounds.

She Knows Me By My Latté

I was sitting in another coffee shop when I heard a man introduce the female barista to his wife.

"She knows me by my latté."

To which the wife replied, to anyone within earshot in a vitriolic tone,

"A lot of people know him by his latté."

A lady who comes in quite regularly and is usually very friendly came in one morning, as per usual, and found us extremely busy. This must not have been acceptable to her that particular morning. She had to wait longer than usual, as often happens during high customer volume. This apparently upset her, which she let us know by yelling that "Everyone was standing around" and no one was getting her coffee, which was untrue. There were several people in front of her who needed to get their coffees first, obviously.

She later came in and apologized for her outburst yet made some claim that she really hadn't been mad at us but rather the customer in front of her who was taking a long time. If this was indeed true, why did she make the accusatory comment about us "standing around?"

While I appreciate her apology, because she is the only customer who has, why in the world did she feel she had to lie about the reason she was mad? If she had stated the real reason, we could have perhaps understood her statement about us "standing around," which to this day I don't. The only people that were "standing around" were the register people, and that is because it is their job to stand there and take orders. Everyone else was hustling around trying to get caught up on orders. I don't understand why people don't realize that they can't expect to get their coffee within two minutes when there is a line going out the door. I seriously doubt she would pull the same stunt in McDonald's. She didn't apologize to the people she had offended directly. Instead she apologized to Michelle, who was the supervisor that day.

I cannot tell you how much I hate it when people stare at me. It is such a huge pet peeve of mine. I always feel as though they are being critical of me, as if what I'm doing isn't good enough. Interestingly enough, my huge repulsion towards this probably stems from the fact that I do it (or used to anyway, until I realized how annoying it is). I always like to look people in the eye when I'm talking and get annoyed if they don't hold my gaze. In those cases I would become sort of an "optic-terrorist," if you will, sort of forcing them to meet my eyes. I never realized how annoying and intrusive this was until I had it done to me. I always fancied holding someone's gaze as intense, confident and somewhat mysterious behavior. Now I don't do it as much because I realize how it can freak someone out. There is a woman named Sylvia who has the look of a crazed madwoman who simply will not loosen her gaze. A few encounters with her were enough to make me want to change my ways.

I was arguing with Alan today, trying to get him to come around and see my side. However, I went about it completely the wrong way. My reptilian brain was working full force. I tried to return his accusations with sarcasm, which, of course backfired on me. One of the cardinal rules of dealing with reptilian behavior is not to be sarcastic or return the attitude. I knew this, but I was just mad because I felt I wasn't being heard. Well, my reptilian behavior was contagious, and boy did he catch it. By the time I had simmered down, he was going full force, reptile-like.

Susan Dunn, MA, [the EQ coach] explains in her article, "There Are Times When We Are Not Open to Reason," "The reptilian brain takes over sometimes; it's there to keep us alive, and its instinctual messages are strong. The limbic brain can also 'flood' us with emotions. Have you used the phrase 'talk 'til you're blue in the face'? These are some of the times when our neo-cortex (thinking brain) shuts down and we "can't be reasoned with.' Unless we know some EQ [emotional intelligence], that is."[20]

What a sight it was to see. Alan wouldn't let me talk, and when he did his posture was as defensive as a brick wall. Both his body language and his verbiage told me that he wasn't the least bit interested in what I had to say. It really wasn't a pretty sight. Witnessing this made me feel so ashamed that I had started it that I had stooped to his level when I knew better. This situation is a living testament to me of our inability to think while in brainstem mode, where your only recourse is to react. Thinking and reasoning are higher brain functions.

I heard a disgusting thing on Oprah the other day. The guest that day was a health inspector of some sort who said that when samples of water were taken from the toilets and the ice machines at certain fast food chains, the ice machine was often dirtier. I'm glad whomever it was didn't come to the Café because that certainly would be the case here.

Can I just say something about interrupting? It is extremely reptilian. Customers (and it's always the same ones) will frequently ask me something else at the exact moment I am trying to relay their order to the appropriate people. I usually just write this off as being rude and ignorant. While it is very annoying, I am able to overlook it, but today, the unthinkable happened. I was in the middle of calling out Marc's ½-caf, double-short soy, no foam, two-sugar latté in the middle of an already chaotic and loud atmosphere when he interrupts to asks me if the large coffee sitting on the counter is his (he had also ordered a drip coffee). When I interrupt his order, mind you, saying "I think so," he interrupts me further by saying, in a slightly annoyed tone, "Well, could you please check?"

This is the height of inscrutability for me. He could obviously hear that I was in the middle of ordering his latté. This was not his first visit to the Café; he knows the drill. I had planned to do (as I always do) this after I was finished ordering his latté, which is the more time-intensive of the two orders to fulfill. I just haven't quite figured out how to carry on two different conversations with two different people yet. I just don't think people realize how insensitive they are being. At least, I truly hope that they don't.

Mind Control?

I just found a really fun way to amuse myself at work. Mind control is not only fun to watch, but being in "control" gives me a sense of power. I already know the power of suggestion, which I use very effectively as a salesperson, but this is something more, a "steering," if you will. It starts with a mistake on my part (or is it?). Melanie gets a black and white mocha, which is my staple drink, except I get it iced. So every time Melanie comes in I say to her "Iced black and white mocha?" She always corrects me and laughs about my always pushing the "iced" on her. (It's just easier; that way I don't have another drink to remember; I already know my drink, after all). This goes on for weeks, nay, months until she comes in, orders it iced, and likes it better! Why people question me, I'll never know.

I've even had instances where I'll suggest something, and they won't like it as much at first. Then one later day it will just get in their head to get it the way I prescribe, and they'll love it. Ah, what a fun puppet show the Café can be.

We have two distinct personality types working in the Café. Alan and Mike are both hard core black and white, (i.e. it's either this way or it isn't and what I perceive to be right is always right.). Melinda, the other manager, is the polar opposite, always giving people the benefit of the doubt. She is extremely considerate of other people's feelings, possibly to her detriment. When Melinda is letting you know that you did something wrong, she is super-sugary nice about it, whereas the other two are overly confrontational, almost as though you did whatever wrong you did as a personal insult to them (which sometimes is fun to do). If you're constantly catching hell for everything, why not have a little fun in the process?

The Café has employees who go away to school and come back in the summer to work. This is great except during the summer the year-round workers get stiffed on hours because there are more people to put on the schedule. This isn't fair to us year-rounder's, I believe. While it's nice to get a little break, unfortunately my bills are still on active duty.

At least this was what I assumed to be the situation because when I asked Alan about why I wasn't getting the hours I needed, he said, "Because I have more staff to work with." However, when I spoke with him the next day, Alan denied that he had even made that statement, getting angry and completely missing the point of what I was saying. (This is an example of not remembering something, due to stress) From the way he reacted, you would have thought I had said "I hate the summer help" and then strategically laid out to him an elaborate murder scheme for them.

Apparently, the summer help are not the ones taking the hours. It is the new assistant manager, who requires a base 40 hours a week. This was not explained to me, or I wouldn't have even mentioned the summer help, both of whom I really like.

Child at Heart

John is a funny little man. He always seems hurried or impatient in the line and will be visibly tapping his foot, sighing, looking at his watch, whatever, until it is his turn. I find this amusing because when he gets up to the register he always takes his time, slowly getting his money out, chatting with us about whatever happened to him yesterday. His love for samples is almost childlike. Here is an over 40-year-old man who will grab handful upon handful of samples, unapologetically. The contrast between the two personalities he displays is comical. He's the busy banker/business-type with a greedy inner child who just can't get enough dessert. As soon as he perceives himself to be in the way, making other customers wait, he gets this sheepish, childlike grin on his face which I dare anyone to get mad at, it's just so adorable.

Tina is the new assistant manager, which is actually a step down for her, as she has managed a couple of stores prior. She was fussing with the deployment Alan had laid out for the day, realizing it didn't really make sense for the day's schedule and most likely wouldn't work. So she was explaining to us how it would work today, over-explaining herself to us two underlings.

"I'm sure whatever you decide will be fine." I laughed.

I had always thought I had a good relationship with our district manager, Bob. I've known him since years back. The funny thing about Bob is that he's very absent from the environment with which he's paid to manage. Several years ago, I had called him to complain about my then-manager who was extremely slacking off and shirking all responsibility. Bob had been clueless to the goings on at that location. When another manager had attempted to complain about the same situation, Bob's response was, "He's been there for two years!" as if that made everything okay and as if the fact that he had stuck it out for so long magically made him into a great manager. That statement should have served as a warning to him that maybe he should be a little more involved.

I encountered a similar problem with Bob myself. Alan reports directly to Bob and tells him about what is going on in the store. Our styles are completely different, as is very evident here. Alan has poisoned his mind toward me because Alan tells Bob only about all the things I do wrong or things he doesn't like, Now Bob doesn't say a thing to me anymore when he sees me. He has a one-sided view of me.

Madge is an attractive 30-something who owns a hip new dating service. Her classy appearance hides the opportunistic desperation that lies just beneath her surface. Mate-Match is very successful, so it's hard to believe she is so greedy.She uses the Café as both her marketing focus group, her "audience." Whenever she comes in, she assaults whoever happens to be within earshot with, "What characteristics do you look for in a potential mate?" "Where do you like to go on a first date?" "Have you ever considered using a dating service?" "Have you ever heard of Mate-Match? It was, after all, voted best dating local service in a 'Best

Of' poll in one of the community papers" and other such questions. She is such an obnoxious promotion monster that people run in all directions when they see her coming for fear that she will try to set them up with someone, which ordinarily might not be so bad except that she charges a $50 introduction fee. "You don't REALLY want to spend the rest of your life ALONE, do you?"

People would often ask me why I never became a supervisor or manger due to my long tenure at the Café. My answer was simply this: "I don't want to be a bitch." I am high-strung enough as it is without having more responsibilities added to my plate. Please don't misunderstand. I would totally be the same way if I were in their position, but probably a lot worse.

Tara is a petite, dainty little southern belle, just as her name implies. She comes across as sweet and charming, but beneath her pristine surface lies a temperament that more closely resembles a boa constrictor. The Café has a refill policy of $.54 if you have your cup. From the looks of it, Tara keeps her same paper cup for weeks on end, just to get the $.54 refill. On one occasion she asked Kelly if she could have another cup, to which Kelly replied that she would then have to charge her the regular price since it would no longer be a refill. This was obviously not the answer that Tara was expecting. She asked (in her sweetest voice, of course) who our district manager was and then said something to the effect of "Oh, I think she was the one who so helpful to me last time." Even this tactic didn't give her the new cup she was expecting.

It is a rare occasion that I could actually sit down and eat lunch with some of my coworkers, but today it happened. A customer joined us and asked us for some dirt on the Café, like what kind of stuff goes on between co-workers that customers aren't privy to. We told him the best way to sum it up was just how much drama goes on in the store. Tami said that it's because there are so many females at the Cafe, and that girls are by nature drama queens. Jenny said that there is probably a lot of jealousy between the "schooled" and "unschooled." While it's probably true that all of these things may play into it, I think the main thing is that it is such a high-stress environment, which of course is going to bring out the worst in human nature.

I truly think that Alan and I speak a completely different language. I can tell him something and he will repeat it back to me so I know that he's heard exactly what I said yet come to a completely different interpretation of it than what I meant. He hears only what he wants to hear (whatever will vindicate him, and make him right). You see, in his mind at least, it is inconceivable that he could ever be wrong. Admitting that you might possibly be wrong is a trait only the strong possess.

Alan shows a distinct insecurity while trying to mask it. He is always pointing out the faults of others, no matter how miniscule, thus making himself seem very together is very much a trait of insecure people. I can say this with complete authority because not only have I seen it a lot, I do and have done it myself quite a bit. It's a common coping mechanism because it works. But only if you do it right. Unfortunately, Alan does it way better than me. He must have years of practice under his belt, which is actually kind of sad when you think about it.

I happened to overhear a conversation between Alan and another co-worker. They were talking about another previous worker, Ken (no longer working with us), who might be called a "problem" employee.

"…no, I didn't have a problem with Ken, but I'll tell you who I absolutely hated was Marshall," I overhear Alan say. Now not only was Marshall my friend, he was the last person I could imagine anyone not liking. There is just nothing unlikable about him.

"Why in the world do you hate Marshall?" I had to ask.

"Our personalities just didn't mix," was Alan's nonchalant answer. I can totally understand why their personalities don't mix. Marshall is completely laid back and not uptight at all. It could possibly be perceived that he doesn't give a rat's ass about anything, but nothing could be further from the truth. Marshall did his job well, probably better since he wasn't so stressed out. Needless to say, I walked away with a clearer understanding of how Alan feels about me, since our personalities certainly don't mix, he must obviously hate me as well.

Reptiles tend to not like non-reptiles. They feed on stress and dislike anything or anyone that hinders their stress.

Overcoming the Reptile

The key to overcoming reptilian behavior, although very obvious, seemingly simplistic, and often the hardest thing, is to get out of "brainstem mode" and start thinking with higher parts of the brain.

There are any number of ways in which people can and do this, probably unbeknownst to them most of the time. Self-talk and what psychologists like to call "reframing" the situation (stepping back, taking an objective look at what is really happening and not what I have blown up in my head) are the primary methods I use to often realize that the situation is not quite as dire as I had originally thought.

I would like to say that I always do this, but the truth is no one does it consistently all the time, though we ALL know what it feels like on the other side when we don't.

Now, as far as I know, no one has ever kicked, bit, spat, thrown, or hit at the Café (not yet, anyway), but the principle is the same. When we are stressed, we tend to go to our base nature, the "me-first' survival mode. I'm sure it's true of any job. We attack first (verbally) and ask questions later. It's part of our biology.

I have found firsthand that reptilian brain is very contagious. When Alan or whoever is acting reptilian, it pisses me off and stresses me out, and then I start acting within my brainstem. Even though I know this, it doesn't change how I react to him, which becomes my problem, not his.

Let me explain: If at any time in your life you have had continuous situations where perhaps you needed a means of "defense," i.e. any kind of abuse, or aggression, whether it's actual or simply perceived, the defense response develops by necessity and is triggered anytime one feels stress, real or imagined.

I observed an interesting event. I was opening with Alan and Mike the other day, when they found that the milk order was lacking. Further investigation showed it to be in a different refrigerator. Closer inspection showed that the temperature in the freezer wasn't high enough. The milk delivery person had obviously checked the temperature and found a refrigerator that was correct to load the milks in, thus preventing spoilage (something way above and beyond his call of duty). During this whole scene, both Alan and Mike were slandering the poor milk guy. After the whole plot had unfolded, Mike admitted, "Actually, that was kind of nice."

But Alan was not to be appeased. "He could have left a note and we STILL need the rest of our order," he thundered to his superior on the phone.

Now I can understand both sides of this. I can imagine it would be very stressful to come in on Monday morning to find that there was a shortage of an extremely necessary product. The milk guy should have left a note, but he also could have just left the milk at the incorrect temperature, thus costing the Café lots of wasted money. Now, I don't know, but my guess is he was probably set behind schedule because of all of the extra work and was in such a hurry that writing a note possibly slipped his mind.

We have a "neighborhood bulletin board" hanging in the Café. I hung up an article, "Pay it Forward," about a drive-through Café where a man got his drink free one day because the baristas had messed up his order, and he had to wait a little longer. The man said if he didn't have to pay, he would pay for the next customer's drink. This started a chain that went on for five more customers.

One day, Jane, one of our regulars, came in and mentioned how nice that was and also how rare it would be for it to happen at our Café. I started laughing when she said, "I wonder how the chain-ending fifth person reacted: 'Oh boy! My lucky day! See ya!'" We both agreed that either one of us would probably have been the one to stop the chain as well.

It finally hit me what Alan's and my problem is. When either of us are questioned (about anything), we take offense simply because we are being questioned. This is ironic because I know how much I hate this behavior in him; I can only imagine that he feels similarly about this behavior in me. Perhaps this is why we clash so much.

I remember I recognized a similar pattern in my relationship with Tracey (previous manager), yet when I pointed it out one day to her she vehemently denied it.

We were arguing one day about something which I don't remember, but it hit me that the problem was that we were too similar. I mentioned it to her not only as a means of trying to quell the argument but also as a way to validate her. This completely backfired on me and only made her angrier. She simply was not willing to hear that she was anything like me when, in her mind, I was so far out in left field. Oh well. It wasn't easy for me to admit it either.

Why, you may ask, am I spending so much time dissecting the nature of stress? It is because stress causes reptile thinking and reptile thinking can be deadly to our everyday wellbeing.

This is not only indicative of witnesses relaying their crime experiences, but it is also true of anyone in any stressful situation. Stress makes you less productive.

The reptilian brain is so contagious that it's probably best to avoid them all together. Leonardo da Vinci gives some valuable advice (probably not with regard to the reptilian brain, but it's applicable). Actually the exact words of da Vinci were, "It's easier to resist at the beginning than at the end."[21] So if you just resist getting sucked in by the reptiles, it makes it easier on you not to be influenced by their reptilian ways.

When I am away from the situation, I can feel sorry for Alan, as he has no doubt been "trained" to use this as a defense mechanism. In The Biology of Violence: How Understanding the Brain, Behavior, and Environment Can Break the Vicious Cycle of Aggression, Debra Niehoff explains that once a person has developed a response system for threat, it is activated by even the smallest stressor.[22]

Training & the Brainstem

Since memory essentially shuts down amidst stress, any training or learning is virtually impossible in such circumstances.

Alan told me that I am "always" accusing him of things he didn't say. However, I usually write down what he says shortly after he says it so that I do remember exactly what he said. It's not surprising that he doesn't recall what he said; memory is the first thing to go when you are stressed. I think that not only is he just not remembering what he said, he probably wouldn't want to admit what he said either.

CONCLUSION

Stress happens. Nothing is going to change that. However it is my hope that, armed with this knowledge, we can begin to change our reactions to it. We should know that no one is perfect and it is impossible to change overnight, but it is possible to take small, baby steps toward treating people better (even when they annoy the crap out of you).

About the Author

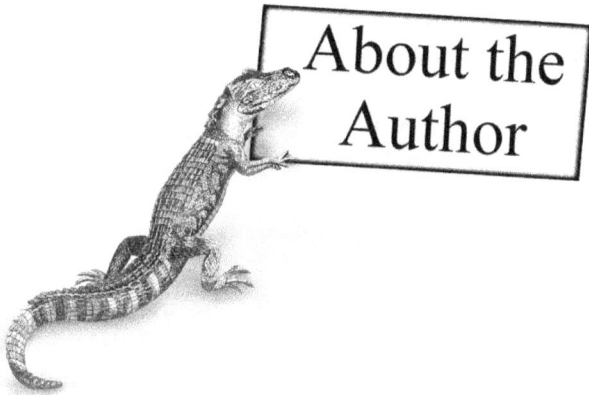

Brooke S. Musterman, a native of Charlotte, NC, has been a barista at several different cafes and coffee shops. She spends her free moments at coffee shops and perfecting her downward dog, but not at the same time.

REFERENCES

1. Susan Dunn, M.A, *Examples of Reptilian Behavior in the Workplace*, © Susan Dunn, M.A., The EQ Coach Published on June 20th, 2006 / Business [online] available www.susandunn.cc

2. Clyde the Goldfish [online] available
http://www.lionden.com/clydes1.htm

3. Dr. Jane Arzt dc The Vitality Center [online] available
http://www.networkvitalitycenter.com/images/new_stress_response_artic le.pdf

4. Debra Niehoff, Ph.D., *The Biology of Violence*, © 1999 Free Press p.83

5. Paul MacLean

6. Babette Rothschild, MSW, LCSW © 1997
Invited article for Soziale Arbeit Schweiz
(The Swiss Journal of Social Work), February 1998.

7. Dr. Suzanne LaCombe, "Activation"c.2006
http://www.myshrink.com/councleing-theory.php?t-id=61

8. David Lee *The Hidden Costs of Trauma In The Workplace* [online] available http://www.humannatureatwork.com/Workplace-Stress-3.htm

9 Jeffrey Gitomer *Little Gold Book of YES! Attitude: How to Find, Build and Keep a YES! Attitude* FT Press; 1 edition 2006 pg. 73

10. Paul Chek, *Balancing the Autonomic Nervous System,* © 2006 The CHEK Institute [online] available
www.chekinstitute.com/articles.cfm?select=68

11. Susan Dunn, M.A *The Tyrannosaurus Rex Rears Its Necessary Head,* © Susan Dunn, M.A., Clinical Psychology, The EQ Coach, [online] available www.salesbrain.net/users/folder.asp?FolderID=6217

12. Dr. Suzanne LaCombe, Ph.D *What's With the Reptile?* © October 9, 2006 [online] available http://www.myshrink.com/reptile.php

13. Terry Bragg, How to deal with clients, bosses, and coworkers who act like reptiles ©2000 All rights reserved Terry Bragg•Peacemakers Training [online] available www.terrybragg.com/Article_Reptilianbrain.htm

14. Mr. Tickles and CJ

15. Victoria Alexander, http://www.filmsinreview.com/At%20Home/tvrev--sopranos.html

16. Dr. Suzanne LaCombe, The Freeze Response c. 2007 http://www.myshrink.com/counseling-theory.php?t-id=66

17. The Innovative Brain *Network But Seriously, nobody's Perfect...or Surrender to Your Humanity*

18. Susan Dunn, MA Clinical Psychology, The EQ Coach *Could 'Willpower' Have Helped Mike Tyson?* © Susan Dunn http://www.susandunn.cc

19. Jeffrey Gitomer *Little Gold Book of YES! Attitude: How to Find, Build and Keep a YES! Attitude* FT Press; 1 edition 2006 pg. 73 pg. 79

20. Susan Dunn, MA Clinicial Psychology, There Are Times When We are Not Open to Reason.

21. Leonardo DaVinci

22. Debra Niehoff, Ph.D., *The Biology of Violence,* © 1999 Free Press p.83

www.ingramcontent.com/pod-product-compliance
Lightning Source LLC
Chambersburg PA
CBHW031522270326
41930CB00006B/478